Mysterious Ways

DISCOVERING THE MIRACLES OF LIFE
AS I FIGHT FOR MY OWN

JAY GITTLESON

Dedication

This book is dedicated to my wife Ellen and my daughter Lizzie who have always believed in me.

Testimonials for **Mysterious Ways**

Jay Gittleson is a unique individual. He's in a personality category all by himself—he's "an attractor." What's an attractor?!

Superstar athletes, famous comedians, inspiring speakers and a whole assortment of interesting people somehow find their way to him. It's almost as if they are magically drawn to him. How does it happen? I don't know. How long has this been happening? For as long as I've known Jay, he's always had this "attractor magic."

Jay's conversations with me usually begin with him saying, "You'll never guess whom I met today."

I've been lucky to have had Jay represent me as a speaker for over 15 years. Through the connections Jay has made throughout his career, he's helped me go places and speak to groups that I never could have dreamed of.

There's only one Jay Gittleson and I'm lucky to have him as a friend.

You're lucky too because now that you have Jay's book in your hands, he's going to share his amazing stories and magic with you!

—Rob Gilbert, Ph.D.

I've known Jay Gittleson for many years and he has always been a beautiful soul, which is why it's so heartwarming to witness the spiritual awakening he's been experiencing in recent years. The diagnosis of any serious health issue can be devastating, and Jay has certainly experienced his share of challenges including questioning God's benevolence. Yet through it all, Jay sought a deeper understanding of his circumstance. He questioned whether there was a greater purpose to his life and in the midst of his own uncertainties and anxieties, Jay found himself reaching out to others to help enrich their lives and alleviate their suffering in any way he could. His focus shifted from his own fears and struggles to the well-being of others, some of whom were perfect strangers.

Join Jay in this remarkably poignant collection of heartwarming stories of life, from the darkness of fear and apprehension to the wisdom and Light to Divine Truth. You will witness the beauty of discovering the inherent value of adversity and the discovery of life's universal purpose.

I am confident that Jay's recollection of his personal experiences will touch your heart as deeply as they did mine.

—Janet Pfeiffer
Author, speaker

Jay and I met a number of years ago after I got in touch with him through my efforts to connect with fellow kidney transplant patients. Since that time, and although he and I have never met in person, I've gotten to know him through a variety of his outreach efforts supporting the transplant community and during many long conversations that he and I have had. Along with learning about Jay's transplant and medical journey, I've also been lucky enough to have him recount to me stories about the diverse people from all walks of life that he's met and their related stories, which he writes about in his book. Jay is a very thoughtful and caring individual with a deep well of emotions that I believe he calls on to inform and support the pursuit of his book and his life in general.

It's been a true honor and pleasure for me to get to know and develop a relationship with Jay.

The connection that he and I have developed has been a wonderful learning experience that has enriched my life and helped me to put better into focus my transplant advocacy efforts. With humbleness I'd say that I'm a better person from having met Jay and certainly the true beneficiary of our relationship.

—Christopher Murphy

Jay's stories are so beautiful and profound. The reason I feel this way is that I believe the stories are interwoven with the Divine. There are many elements in this short life that in fact "connect" us! I have had the distinct privilege to watch how some of these marvelous moments have unfurled in Jay's life! For example, Jay told me that when he was first on dialysis he wondered if it was God's way of "punishing him." However, as I watched Jay go through these amazing trials life had designed for him, I noticed a transformation. He went from a wildly questioning, uneasy being to a calm, resolute persona. Sometimes the Divine can change us, heal us from the perceptions we carry. This is a great gift. Jay not only has "connected" in a profound way with so many people but has helped many people along his path. He has raised a spotlight and given a microphone to others his whole life. He has watched from behind the scenes, never fully feeling he should take just a moment for himself in that spotlight.

I am so proud to call Jay a friend. I am so proud that he finally realized that he and his stories are so important that it is time to shine the spotlight on Jay and on these wonderful, compelling, true stories. God Bless you, Jay! If people feel these stories anywhere near as deeply moving as I have, this book will reach people's hearts and souls!!

—Billy Ayres, founder
Lifeline Theatre & Arts Center

I have tried to recreate events, locales and conversations from my memories of them. To protect privacy, in some instances I have changed the names of individuals and places.

CONTENTS

Editor's Note

Before I began to edit Jay's memoir, he and I had several emotionally strong conversations about his book and the extraordinary connections he has made in his life. Jay is an outgoing, big-hearted man who has a deep desire to get to know people and help them in any way he can. As such, people gravitate toward him, open their hearts, and share their remarkable stories with him.

In our conversations, Jay and I bonded over a mutual fascination with writer Mitch Albom, the *Detroit Free Press* sports columnist who went on to author many bestsellers such as *Tuesdays with Morrie*. Jay and I greatly admired Albom's writing style, specifically his ability to bring out the personality, humanity, and emotional impact of the men and women he writes about. When Jay and I were younger writers, Albom inspired both of us to "touch" readers in similar ways.

During our phone conversations, before I read his manuscript, Jay and I discussed how to organize the chapters in this book. I told him just to send me the chapters in non-chronological order, in a sequence that simply felt right to him. He did so, and it was the right decision.

Throughout my edit of Jay's manuscript, I felt transported back to the late 1980s, when I read *The Live Albom*, a seemingly scattered collection of Mitch's best *Free Press* columns, but with a thread of humanity connecting the stories. It was a warm, sometimes melancholy, and often joyful reading experience.

I did not have a similar experience until 34 years later, while reading Jay's collection of life stories in this remarkable book. Whether it's the story of the sweet-hearted dancer who offered to donate a kidney to Jay, or the day he held hands in prayer with Pastor Darryl Strawberry, or a toast of gratitude from Jay's good friend "Mike the Clown," these indelible stories surprise, inspire, and pull at the heartstrings.

I hope you are moved as much as I was by *Mysterious Ways*.

—David Aretha

Foreword
Jay's Journey of Hope

By Ellis Henican

I t is impossible to count all the people Jay Gittleson has inspired, just like we'll never know all the lives he has helped to change. As a teacher.

As a public speaker.

As a business owner and community leader.

As a father, husband, colleague, mentor, and friend.

And now as the author of this life-changing book.

That's what happens when you dedicate your life to "making a difference" in the lives of those around you. People look to you when they need a lift, even when they don't know how badly they can use one, which is true for all of us sometimes.

Some people go through life asking, "What can you do for me?" A few rare souls—and Jay is one of them—don't even ask, "What can I do for you?" They just do it. For people like Jay, the pleasure comes in the giving. They don't even wait around for thanks.

I met Jay through Dwight Gooden, the brilliant and troubled Major League pitcher. Dwight and I wrote a book together about his tumultuous journey through New York and baseball, which is to say through life. Thank God Dwight's story has a happy ending. He and I were out telling it when Jay stepped up to help. Without even being asked, he brought Dwight's uplifting message to audiences who otherwise never would have heard it, passing on the good news and changing another set of lives.

Who is this man for others? Where does he get his power and his influence? How has he built a life around giving instead of taking? How has he done so well at doing good?

I wondered too. At last, all those answers are here.

Starting his career in the public classrooms of New York City. Launching his own speakers agency two months before the 9/11 terror attacks, just when inspiration was needed most. Deciding after becoming a father that the world had enough takers already. What it needed was more people who were ready to give.

There's a roadmap for living here…for anyone bold enough to follow it.

And there's also a twist. It's a big one. The day would come when Jay became the one in need. It was life-or-death this time, and that wasn't just an expression. The stakes were the highest imaginable, and there was no middle ground.

Would all that giving that Jay had done flow back in his direction? Would he get the glorious payback he so richly deserved—call it faith, call it karma, call it whatever you like? No one who knew Jay ever doubted his energy or his resolve, even though the odds this time were stacked heavily against him.

I won't spoil the story for you. I can't tell it nearly as well as Jay can, every heart-pounding twist and turn.

I will only say this much: Among the many lives that Jay has changed, now there is another one.

His own.

If we'll only open our hearts, his inspiring story will change ours too.

My Life:
What I've Experienced,
What I've Learned

As I faced end-stage renal failure in 2015, I was extremely saddened at the prospect of not being able to see my daughter Lizzie grow into womanhood and see her life unfold. I told a nurse educator, "Why is God punishing me?" She responded vigorously, "Don't you say that! God is a loving God!"

A kidney transplant was needed, but dialysis was my only option as I had ballooned to almost one hundred pounds over the BMI weight requirement to qualify to get on the deceased donor kidney waiting list. I had made it to the operating room doors for bariatric surgery a year earlier. However, the surgery was aborted after the early morning blood test showed that my condition had worsened and it was too risky to move forward. I knew God was watching over me as I'd never wanted that procedure.

The doctor told me it was time to start dialysis. I refused to start until I had a surprise Sweet Sixteen party for Lizzie. The doctor told me, "You must start immediately after that." Calls from the office were streaming in for me to report to dialysis. I then told them, "I will start right after my daughter's last high school swim meet for the season." I stood dizzy and drained on the balcony of the hot pool that day as I saw my daughter make a personal best. I shouted over the railing to the coach, "Did you see that? Did you see that! That's my daughter." My shouts were drowned out by all the shouting and cheering for the next race, but my daughter saw and heard me.

When I reported for dialysis the next day, the physician assistant said, "Sure, you will be that one in a million who will lose the weight on your own. You should still get bariatric surgery." I was determined to be that one in a million.

I decided to stay positive. I was forty-seven years old and surrounded by much older and in many cases sicker people who might not ever qualify for a transplant. I wanted to get to know the patients and staff who would soon become like family to me.

My life proved to be full of miracles. In this book, you will read about how I went to college straight out of a psych ward after a court case with my father, became a teacher, got married, and had a miracle daughter on 01-01-01 who inspired me to start a motivational speakers bureau.

I've made miracle connections with people who have saved my life, including celebrities like my childhood sports hero. I even had a thirty-year friendship with a homeless man who mentored me in the subway. In kidney failure, I moved my family to a Pennsylvania town called Nazareth. We were led to an evangelical Christian church, whose congregation later worked hand in hand with orthodox rabbis who came to Nazareth to help save my life. The outpouring of support from both friends and strangers during my search for a living kidney donor was such a blessing in my life. At the same time, I became engaged in helping and encouraging others along their journeys both in and out of the dialysis room, which enriched me and helped me to grow as a person.

Just before I started dialysis in 2016, I unexpectedly received a message from a woman named Maria who had been looking for me for nearly three decades. She asked me about my life. I sensed, though, that she had something profound to share with me. Why was she looking for me all those years, and what did she want to tell me? She also made me think about the people I would look for in my life. Soon after, I made a list of thirty-seven people whom I wanted to find, whom I felt had made a positive impact on me during my life. I launched my "Reconnection Tour" while on dialysis, including my reconnection with Maria. What she told me changed my life forever.

I have had a challenging life that has included family traumas, abandonment, and major health issues. At the same time, I have lived a life filled with wonderful, serendipitous encounters with remarkable people who have revealed themselves as my points of light through some dark times. I have been blessed to meet people like my college roommate, who became a Grammy-nominated singer and toured the world with Mariah Carey, and a high school friend who became an NBA head basketball coach. I have had strong encounters and connections with professional comedians and actors, such as Fred "Rerun" Berry, and famous athletes, including Manute Bol, Dwight Gooden, and Darryl Strawberry. I tell these stories in the pages of this book.

I was also blessed to know a compulsive gambler who was a father figure, a provocative homeless man who became my longtime buddy, and a former rock musician who played one last show, for my family, just before he died. These human beings whom I have met on my life's path have guided my character and given me hope and a positive outlook. In my journey, I've discovered that God indeed works in mysterious ways.

Gains and Losses

I started to feel intense pain in my side one night just before Thanksgiving in 2015. My daughter, who had just started her freshman year of high school, was the only one home in Nazareth and had already gone to bed. The pain was getting more and more intense on my right side. I was doubled over in the upstairs hallway. I did not want to call 911 and cause a major ruckus.

I called a friend named Luis around midnight. He was the only person I knew so far in the area where we had just moved to. We had met at a YMCA swim team training that our kids had participated in. I said, "Luis, I am sorry to bother you but I am in a lot of pain."

Without hesitation Luis said, "My wife and I will come right over. It will take us like thirty minutes to get to you. If the pain gets worse just call 911."

I was crying a little bit at that point and said, "I will wait for you." I often got emotional and had flashbacks of the tough times in my life where I had been at the brink, left to my own devices, and felt alone. There was always a feeling inside of me that there was something I still needed to accomplish in my life. The recurring thought of my daughter being left behind without a father hurt so much.

Luis and Fabiola left their teenaged kids home asleep and drove over at midnight to see what they could do to help. I was in so much pain that they decided to take me to a local emergency room. Fabiola held my hand on the way to the hospital in the back seat as the pain further intensified.

After a CAT scan revealed that I was bleeding internally, Fabiola insisted that they stay with me until I was admitted, which was not until 3:00 a.m. I was very scared because the emergency room doctor informed me that if the bleeding did not stop on its own, a surgical procedure would need to be done. Contrast dyes used in the process could jeopardize what little kidney function I had left. The fistula in my arm, my future access point for dialysis, had been created just a month earlier and was not yet mature enough to be utilized. If I needed dialysis right away, doctors would need to insert a chest catheter with all the accompanying risks that I had hoped to avoid.

I was up all night after I was admitted and taken upstairs. I was so uncomfortable on the hard rubber mattress in an otherwise pleasant-looking private room. I could not get comfortable with the pain in my side, and my lower back was aching.

I imagined my daughter waking up and wondering what had happened to me when she was getting ready for school. I later found out that she ran out to catch the school bus and never even noticed I was gone, which was probably for the best anyway. My wife was living in a small apartment close to her job in New Jersey and was unaware of my situation.

An Indian woman doctor visited me that morning and told me that they would scan my abdominal region each day to see if the bleeding stopped on its own. I was weak and tired and my hemoglobin level was steadily dropping as I kept losing blood.

I took the blanket and found a narrow place alongside the window to lay down on my opposite side to relieve the pressure on my back. A nephrologist came to see me and explained that it was still a wait-and-see proposition. He did not belong to the kidney practice or hospital system to which I belonged so I was not able to communicate directly with my regular doctors. I felt so alone. My wife did not have any sick days left and continued working. It was the week leading up to Thanksgiving. Her sister-in-law went to stay with my daughter.

I prayed for the internal bleeding to stop. On the third and fourth day, scans seemed to confirm that in fact the bleeding had stopped on its own. I spent Thanksgiving Day by myself. I hoped to see someone. I only received a hospital tray with a thin piece of turkey deli meat. A candy striper passed by my room, but I was too weak to yell out as she passed by in the hallway. I was getting weaker and weaker from the blood loss.

On the fifth morning the woman doctor leaned over my bed and pressed a clipboard close to my face and said, "You need to sign this paper giving us consent to give you a blood transfusion." I had read that a blood transfusion and the accompanying antibodies that would be formed in my blood could lessen or eliminate my chances for a kidney donor match. "What about getting a transplant down the line?" I asked the doctor. She looked at me compassionately and tried to reassure me by saying, "We will spin the blood beforehand. Don't worry. You need to sign this now if you want to make it to transplant one day." I scribbled my signature on the paper.

A couple of hours later the bag of blood arrived and it was placed up on the IV stand. A nurse tried repeatedly to put an IV in my arm but could not find a vein. Multiple people came in and stuck my arm over and over. They tried about forty times. My right arm was off limits due to the fistula, which made it a limb restriction for IVs, blood draws, and blood pressure checks. Eventually the blood went bad from sitting for more than two hours while they tried and tried again on my left arm. An order was made for more blood.

My arm was battered, sore, and swollen. An older woman nurse came into my room suddenly and ordered everyone out. She was yelling, "Get the hell out of here." She turned off the lights in the room. The image of Mr. Miyagi from the movie scene from *The Karate Kid* came to mind where he claps his hands together in the locker room before healing the boy's leg so that he can continue with the competition. This was my "Mr. Miyagi" moment. The nurse said, "I have ten minutes until the end of my shift. Let's do this!"

She pulled the rolling tray table to the side of my bed, lifted my arm up, extended it, and inserted the IV on the first try. I was helped to a recliner and when the blood arrived it was connected to start the flow. Just a few minutes into the process, a woman walked in unexpectedly and said that she needed to take my blood pressure. I was weak and tired. I mustered up all the energy I had and said, "Please no…patient refused," as she proceeded to put the blood pressure cuff over the IV on my left arm right over the transfusion site. I begged her to stop but she inflated the cuff and the IV ruptured into my arm and ended my transfusion.

I was in so much pain and yelled out, "Why did you do that?" The woman ran out of the room. Looking back now, though, she may have saved my life because I never received the full transfusion and that may very well have made my future transplant match possible.

Supernatural Connection

New message" popped up on my cell phone in the spring of 2016. The message flashed in front of me. "My name is Maria. I am looking for someone I met back in 1989 at the Pavilion Hospital. If this is the wrong person, I apologize in advance. But I met someone by this name many years ago and he wrote to me and I was never able to get in touch with him after that. Might that be you? If not, I am sorry. Have a blessed day."

I was taken aback. I knew that I was there in 1989. It would have to be someone that I knew. I responded and said, "I was there, but I am not sure if I remember you."

I received a quick reply. "Good evening, Jay. This is Sara, Maria's daughter. I'm going to be typing for her because she's not too computer savvy. She always tells me stories about her experience there. She remembers you quite fondly, as a very nice young man she used to talk to about God all the time. The Jay that she remembers is Jewish and would always talk about his parents. My mother asked me to search for you and said she has been looking for you for many years."

I did remember a Hispanic woman sitting with me in the hallway of the hospital praying with me. I typed back. "I am the Jay you are looking for."

Sara said, "We are amazed to find you and want to know more." She had a lot of questions from her mom. "My mom had not understood exactly why you were there. She always wondered why this 19-year-old kid was sitting in the hallway of the hospital and why you had no visitors."

I began to tell them my story, and the memories of 1989 came flooding back to me. I told Sara, "It was a difficult period in my life." Sara was translating every word for her mother as I typed.

* * *

"In the Spring of 1989, I was making plans to try to go to college the following Fall. I had been a ping pong ball between living with my father, who basically neglected me, and my mother who, every time I would get back to her, would not want me. All I wanted to do was go to college. I was a straight A student and had never touched drugs or alcohol.

"My father was a college professor. I decided my best option would be to attend his university. All he had to do was sign some tax forms for free tuition for his son. I had already earned a Presidential Scholarship, so room and board was covered. He did not want to sign those papers and it seemed like he wanted nothing to do with me.

"I was told that I was entitled legally to the education that my father could provide for free. One lawyer told me, 'You're smart, but you don't have any money to afford me. You can do it yourself. It is a slam dunk case. Legal Aid will give you some sample forms and instructions. Good luck.'"

I did just that. It took me a couple of months to put together. My mother was the litigant in reopening the divorce settlement. She just needed to sign the papers after I drafted all the documents to set the wheels in motion. Then the case could be heard by a judge. I hoped maybe then I would be able to go to college. My mother was not thrilled with the idea of seeing her ex-husband again in court. My mother would not sign the documents without her demands being included. All I wanted to do was to go to college.

Three weeks before the court date I was on my way home from visiting an old high school friend in New Jersey. As I waited for the downtown bus at 178th Street and Fort Washington Avenue in Manhattan, a taxi pulled up to the curb and this woman rolled down the window and shouted, "Hey Jay!" I was startled.

It was a friend of my mother's and she waved frantically for me to come over to the car. I leaned in to see what she wanted. I thought maybe she was going to offer me a ride downtown. Her face looked pained and concerned. "Get in! get in!" she said, "Your mother has been in a very serious accident and we need to get to the hospital right away." The friend would not tell me what had happened so I prepared for the worst.

I remember like it was yesterday. I said to myself, *Now is your time to be a man. You have no one now if your mother doesn't make it. You are going to have to take control and prepare to take care of everything now. My father abandoned me. My brother abandoned me. If I'm alone now, this is it.*

We arrived at the emergency room. I told the guard that my mother had been in an accident and to please tell me what was going on. I was told someone would be with me in a minute. I just remember thinking "hold it together" and suddenly, a police officer came out to the waiting room. I was really concerned about what he was about to tell me, but then several more officers came out and made a circle around me. One cop told me to take off my belt and empty my pockets. I knew now that this was a charade that my mother had concocted.

I still tried to stay calm and asked to speak to an attorney. This burly cop said, "You'll be coming with us. Give us your belt and your belongings."

A nurse appeared and said, "Oh, don't worry, you just have to stay overnight and you'll settle this with the doctor in the morning. Just explain your story then, but we do need to hold you."

Before I went through this door escorted by all these cops, I turned and glanced down this hallway and I saw my mother standing against the wall next to a soda machine. It looked like she had been crying and was dabbing her eyes with a tissue. I had seen that lost, desperate expression on her face before, which had often led to decisions that were not necessarily in my best interests. She was an intelligent and often convincing person who had made up a story, according to the people there, that I had threatened to jump off the Empire State Building to end my life.

Just an hour earlier, I had been eating a slice of pizza calmly with my friend Jerry in New Jersey before he walked me to the bus stop. For some reason, I half-joked with him, "If my mother ever does anything crazy again to me, will you come to save me?" Jerry said, "What are you talking about? But yeah, of course, Jay."

I went behind the door and into a room marked "psychiatric holding area." No phone calls were allowed, but I convinced the nurse to call Jerry. When he answered, he thought I was pranking him and hung up. The nurse called back and told him I was not joking.

The next morning, I was transported to the Pavilion. I couldn't wait to talk to someone and explain everything. I sat quietly in the hallway of the newly minted Pavilion hospital ward waiting to speak with the doctor. A short, stocky, smiley man in his early thirties appeared in front of me. "I'm Dr. H." He asked me many questions, but he made me feel comfortable. Dr. H said, "We are not going to put you on any medication. We will observe you and I will speak to your mother and try to settle this whole thing." He said they could not discharge me to the street. I had no money or belongings or anything. I was just waiting on a decision from a judge in my case so that I could go free to the college.

I sat on a chair in the hallway outside of this large nurses' station while awaiting further instructions from the staff. It was an eerily quiet psych ward, which had apparently just opened in this new hospital building. I did not see too many staff or patients around. I was wearing blue jeans, sneakers, and a T-shirt with my favorite pistachio green windbreaker. My hair was disheveled and I had taken off my preppie round-rimmed eyeglasses to wipe my eyes from crying in the session with Dr. H. I was so upset with my mother for what she had done that I told the doctor it felt like I had "acid tears."

Just then a Hispanic woman who looked to be in her late thirties appeared in front of me. She had long black hair pulled into a ponytail with thick eyeglasses and a kind, concerned face. I looked up at her and she peered back at me as if she wanted to ask me something.

I said, "Hello, how are you? What is your name?"

"I no speak too much Ingles," she said. "My name es Maria." She studied my face, but she seemed unsure of what I was doing sitting there. I started to cry. She sat down next to me and took my hand. "Let's pray," she said. Maria closed her eyes and prayed out loud in Spanish. I closed my eyes too and clutched her hand. At the end of the prayer, she asked me, "Where is your mother?"

I told her, "My mother does not want me."

Then tears started streaming down her face and Maria said, "Everyone needs a mother."

I asked her, "Will you be my mother?"

My mother did not agree to take me back home. I had nowhere to go. The doctor would say, "We can't discharge you to the street." Each day I sat in the hallway across from the locked door, which led to the main hallway and elevators to the lobby of this small full-service hospital.

One day around lunchtime I saw Maria scurry down the hall-way toward me. She eagerly sat next to me and held my hand to pray with me. Her hand was very warm this time and I felt something strange come over me. It was a feeling of hope and inspiration. For a few moments I lost contact with my body and there was a comfort beyond Maria's hand. I seemed to lose track of time and space. Maria released my hand and looked at me with a sort of wonder in her eyes. I reached for her hand again, but her expression then looked almost apologetic. That feeling in her hand was gone.

About two weeks or so later Maria was discharged. She gave me her home address scribbled on a piece of notebook paper. I promised to stay in touch.

That night, I decided to write a letter to the judge who was handling my case to decide if my father should fulfill his legal responsibility and sign the papers so that I could go to college.

Dear Judge Sorkow,

There are acts of omission and there are acts of commission. My father omitted me and my mother tried to commit me. All I want to do is go to college. I am locked in this place with nowhere to go. They will not discharge me to the street. What can you do to help me?

Judge Sorkow, who had gained a lot of notoriety for his decision in a high-profile case called "Baby M," ruled in my favor. I wrote another letter and mailed it to Maria letting her know of the good news. I went off to college straight out of a psychiatric ward.

***

I told them that I had planned to write a book about my life. Sara interjected, "My mother and I will definitely come to your book signing when you publish it. This is some story." I explained to Sara and Maria that my kidneys were failing and I was quite ill. Dialysis treatment would be necessary in my near future. They wished me well and said that they would pray for me.

⁂

In 2018 I felt it was time to reconnect with Maria in person. I had already been on dialysis for a year. I arranged to travel to see her again. I was greeted at the door by Maria, now in her late sixties, and her wonderful husband, Tony, who had prepared a Dominican feast of chicken, salad, and rice and beans. I again sat with Maria. We held hands and prayed while sitting on her sofa in her living room. I asked her to recall and explain what had happened in 1989 at the hospital that day when we prayed together before her discharge.

Maria described in great detail what she remembered from the hospital. She said, "I used to talk to you about God and about Jesus, but Jay, you told me, 'Oh, I believe in God, but Jesus? I am Jewish.'"

She then proceeded to tell me an extraordinary story about the moment I felt that strange feeling at the hospital—that feeling of hope and inspiration. "Then there was that day," she said. "I was in my room praying with the radio and they were preaching about seeing the glory of God. The preacher said, 'Wherever you are, you're going to see the glory of God. You're going to shine.' I started praying with that preacher on the radio. I put my hands on the radio and the power of God came over me. I went to the floor and when I stood up, I saw the glory of God. That big light. It was shining everywhere in my room and I said, 'Oh, my lord…oh, my God!' I went to the Bible that was on the little table and opened it up right to Isaiah 60: 'Arise, shine because the glory of God came over you.' I didn't know what to do. So, I went into the hallway and went up to you and I said, 'God bless you, Jay.' I didn't know what else to say so I took your hand and you started shaking from head to toe.

God is Not a Feeling.
It's a Knowing

"I said, 'Oh my lord.' God touched you that day, Jay. That experience was for you so it was like electricity over you. I will never forget that. You were shaking and then when you stopped you wanted to give me your hand again because you said you wanted that feeling again. But it was God. That experience that I had was for you. It was only you that was supposed to receive that power. That's the power of God. He touched you and I knew that God had something special for you. God only does that for people that he chooses and if he has some special thing with that person. I know that God has something with you."

Maria took a long, deep breath and then said, "I went home from the hospital a few days later. I don't remember how long after that I received a letter from you and you said you went to college to study. I was so happy. I really had no more contact with you after that. I kept that letter that you sent me for a long time. We moved to the Bronx in 1991. I never heard from you again."

She continued, "I was trying to find you on the computer but I wrote your last name wrong. I couldn't find it and then this one day we were talking about you and Sara said, 'Let me see. He's Jewish, right? Try again to spell his Jewish last name.' All I knew was that it started with the letter G. Was it Gittelsun? Gittlesawn? Gettleson? Sara started looking in the phone book. Then she started looking on the computer. After many months of looking on the computer she said, 'How about this one?' I saw your picture and I said, 'Yes, I think it's him!' It had been a long time, but I knew it was you. Sara had found you."

The phone rang in Maria's apartment just as she finished sharing this vivid memory of what had happened at the hospital. It was Sara. Maria handed me the phone. "Jay," Sara told me on the phone. "I'm so sorry that I couldn't be there to meet you today. I just started a new job as a social worker. Can I share something important with you?" I could tell by the sound of her voice that it was serious. "My mom didn't want to say anything to worry you, but she is sick. Her kidneys are failing. Her doctor told us that she will have to start dialysis. She doesn't want to do it. Can you talk to her and convince her? If you can't do it nobody can."

I was really shocked to hear this news. I looked across the room at Maria. We now had something else in common. Before I left, I spoke to Maria and her husband and we prayed together. Maria gave me a small Bible as a gift.

Over the next year, Maria and I spoke to each other on the phone from our respective dialysis centers. When she had complications and was hospitalized, I visited her and prayed with her.

I qualified to get on to the kidney transplant waiting list, and started a Facebook page to share my story with the hopes of finding a living kidney donor. Maria's daughter informed me that, although she was a willing donor for her mom, Maria did not qualify medically to receive a transplant.

All I could think of at that moment was to open that little Bible that Maria had given me. It opened right to this passage: Isaiah 60: "Arise, shine, for your light has come, and the glory of the LORD rises upon you. See, darkness covers the earth and thick darkness is over the peoples, but the LORD rises upon you and his glory appears over you. Nations will come to your light, and kings to the brightness of your dawn."

I finally understood the significance as to why Maria had searched for me all those years to share the experience of our supernatural connection in the hallway of that hospital in 1989. It gave me a sense of peace in looking back on my life with some perspective. I feel that God had a plan for me. Even through the painful times, there was always a life preserver thrown out to me in the form of a person or event that took place to keep me going and to be able to look back on and draw strength and happiness from. The speakers bureau I started after my daughter Lizzie was born -A Vision in Motion- seemed to have been the manifestation of her "vision" in providing inspirational speakers for over 2 million school kids and youth on life-changing topics.

Maria said to me, "I didn't understand why I had to go to the hospital for forty days and forty nights in 1989. But I think it was because God wanted to touch you and had plans for you. I am one hundred percent sure. That's why he permitted that you go to the hospital. Sometimes the way God chooses to touch somebody is not maybe the way you like it. But it's the way that he chose to touch you and meet you.

"I don't remember anybody else there at the hospital. I don't remember the names or faces of anybody else but you. Only you. I remember you laughing. I remember you saying that your mother didn't want you. At first, I didn't believe you. But then I knew that was true. When God has plans with somebody, he always finds a way to get to that person.

"He wants you to finish your book. That book is going to bless a lot of people. Maybe they're going through trouble. Maybe they don't believe or maybe they need some testimony that God is real. That's why sometimes when you get down or depressed, I ask God, 'Please touch Jay in a way that he has the strength and wisdom to finish that book.' It's going to be a blessing for a lot of people— Jewish and non-Jewish. He has a vision with that book."

Light always overcomes darkness.

Unorthodox Therapy

After a routine blood test in 2007, it was discovered that my kidneys had been damaged by a mental health medication that had been prescribed years earlier. What followed were many doctor appointments and diagnostic tests. I experimented with various treatments as I was weened off the medication, which had damaged the tubules in my kidneys.

I had gone to college and graduate school and had a first career as a teacher on that medication. I had produced comedy shows and then started a meaningful company on that medication. I got married and had a daughter on that medication. I was scared to go off the medication years earlier. What would happen to me and would I lose it all?

It was not long afterward that I fell into a very deep depression. No one really knew what I was going through. The cloud of the 2008 financial crisis loomed overhead as my worries and anxiety consumed me. After I left my teaching job in 2001 after the birth of my daughter, I started a motivational and inspirational speakers bureau for schools. Those programs were the first things cut from school budgets.

My mother-in-law, who lived with us, was dying of cancer at home in hospice. I felt like I was dying right alongside her. The hospice nurse continued to make her routine weekly visits. I wanted to say to the nurse, "I'm probably not going to make it either. Can you comfort me too?" So many forces, both internal and external, were pulling me down.

One evening, on my routine drive home from the doctor's office, my eyes were drawn to a flashing pink neon sign. I unexpectedly turned into the parking lot and went inside. The loud thumping music helped to drown out my thoughts as my eyes scanned the dimly lit room. I wondered if there was someone there I knew who would recognize me. I thought to myself that they could never mention seeing me without others knowing where *they* had been. I just wanted someone to talk to. I went to the bar and ordered a bottle of water.

I was sitting there alone for a few minutes and a petite brunette came over to me and started up a conversation. She said, "What are you doin' drinking water? You come to a place like this and order a bottle of water?" She was a real spitfire and a no-nonsense type of person.

I responded cautiously, "I don't drink." Without missing a beat, she asked me, "What are you, an alcoholic?" I explained that I just never drank my entire life. She said that her name was Stacey and she ordered a vodka with cranberry juice.

She had a slim yet curvy figure with shoulder-length dark brown straight hair. I looked briefly into her impatient dark brown eyes. There was a story in those eyes. She smelled fruity and floral. Her purplish glossy lipstick looked freshly applied. Her makeup was precise, but a little overdone and exaggerated.

She put her hand on my knee and I glanced down. My eyes traveled upward to make eye contact again as I wondered if she could feel the vibrations under her hand. It felt like my leg was responding to thousands of tiny bee stings pricking my skin.

Her Staten Island accent annoyed me, but also endeared her to me. I could hear right through her roughness into a layer of sweetness. That "tell it like it is" personality was her charm. She grabbed my hand and said, "Let's go in the back for a dance."

I nearly fell out of the high bar stool and tried to regain my composure. I said, "I don't dance."

Stacey led me to a semi-secluded room in the back of the club. "I'm the only one who's gonna dance, silly. Just come on."

We went in the back and she started twirling around and biting her lip. I was a bit overwhelmed. I asked her, "How did you come to work here?"

Stacey stopped dancing in front of me and said, "You wanna talk. That's it?" I was nervous that she might just leave me there. The music was loud and it was hard to hear each other. She wiggled in between my legs and sat on my thigh and glared into my eyes. I leaned in to hear what she was about to say. "You're paying for this dance and you just wanna talk?" I could smell her minty breath with a tinge of the vodka mixed in. I could tell she felt sort of safe with me. I really did just want to talk.

She grabbed her oversized Louis Vuitton pocketbook and said, "Let's go!" and escorted me back to my high bar stool and the bartender brought me another bottle of water while Stacey disappeared into the dressing room.

To my surprise, about ten minutes later, Stacey returned to sit with me. The club was almost empty at that point. There was a loud group of disheveled guys in business suits on the other side of the bar who were way too drunk for their own good. While two bouncers escorted them outside, Stacey turned to me and said, "When you walk in here, it's like anything goes in a way. You don't know who you're going to meet or who you're going to talk to or what whack job's going to walk through that door. At the same time, you can meet amazing good people and I definitely think this job has changed my life in many ways."

I asked, "How do you handle drinking all night long?"

"I never drink to the point where I am stupid drunk," she said. "In this business you really have to be on point because anything can happen."

"What did you do before?" I asked.

She said, "I used to work as an aide in a nursing home but it was hard to pay my bills." Her voice cracked a little as she spoke. "When you're in a situation where you don't have any more options, sometimes..." Stacey looked down briefly and said, "God puts you in those situations to kind of make you eat your own words."

I asked, "What do you mean by that?"

She said, "I was one of those people that was very stereotyping and judged people who worked in places like this." I nodded that I understood and she continued.

"I'm not embarrassed that I work here, but when you go to work in a place like this you have to kinda be somebody else. No matter what issues you're having in life, you have to walk through that door and keep your head high and have a smile on your face because you are the entertainment at the end of the day."

It was kind of amazing how open Stacey was with her thoughts and feelings. I just listened. She went on to say, "I mean pretty much this job is definitely draining on somebody. It can definitely wear them out and stuff 'cause they expect so much from you and they gotta realize at the end of the day you're still a person. You're still somebody's daughter, or somebody's mom or somebody's wife or girlfriend or whatever."

My heart sank for her as she added, "It's mentally draining 'cause you know that a lot of guys that come in here are married or have children or are going through a divorce or getting married. So, they're in here doing whatever they want to do. It kind of fucks with your head a little bit in the sense of relationships because then you think all men are like this. These guys are doctors and lawyers and very professional men so it makes you question everything."

The club was about to close for the night and she told me that she was going to cash out with her manager. I left a tip for the bartender and headed out. I tried to make a quick exit. When I reached the lobby, I felt someone behind me so I held the door. When I turned around it was Stacey. I took a double-take as she was so tiny without those giant heels on. She was wearing gray sweatpants, white high-top sneakers, and a gold sparkly hoodie. It was awkward but at the same time we had sort of just become friends.

Over the next two years I would stop in from time to time for a bottle of water and look for her. I knew she could take care of herself in the world, but somehow, I wanted to be part of her doing something better for her life. I encouraged her to go back to school.

She mentioned that she used to take care of this old guy at the nursing home and he became sort of attached to her and vice versa. I became attached to her as well. Our talk sessions usually were late-night encounters. Sometimes she was busy taking care of other guys. I saw her do lots of talking and drinking with them so I guess they became attached to her as well.

Stacey had become my unofficial therapist. She sat at the bar with me and just talked. Sometimes, I was very positive and upbeat and other times down in the dumps. She did try to diagnose me one night. "Jay, you're freaking bipolar." I never told her about my kidneys that were slowly failing.

We shared the same dream. Both of us wanted to write the story of our lives. She asked me how to go about that. I told her that she could call my free conference-call number and tell me the story and I would record it and then transcribe it for her. I didn't think she would call, but she did. She reflected on the choices that she had made in her life up to that point.

Our friendship was based on mutual respect. We only saw

each other in this fake world from time to time. Stacey had real self-esteem amidst the plastic world of women who competed for the attention of strange men. She could look at her situation as necessary, but temporary. She had great insights into things and I learned a lot from her.

I saw a big banner flapping in the breeze outside of the club one night as I drove home. It said, "Stacey's Farewell Party." She had decided to "retire" and move on. I was very happy for her. I went in to say goodbye. She said, "I want to have one last 'dance' with you." She pulled her stool next to mine, leaned in, and she gently kissed me on the lips. Another patron saw what she did and said to a woman sitting at the bar, "How come you don't kiss me like she did him?"

Two years later in 2012, I got a surprise call out of the blue from Stacey. I was shocked when she said, "I finished writing my life story and want to read you the first chapter."

I listened intently. It was heartbreaking as she described some of the traumas of her life. We were on the phone for over an hour and then suddenly she just finished reading. She said, "Goodbye," and hung up. I felt inside that I had made some sort of positive impact on her. She had followed through on her writing goal and I was thrilled that she had reached out to me.

* * *

Years later, in 2018, I was already on dialysis. I was at Dr. H's office in the waiting room on a non-dialysis day and my phone rang. I quickly reached to silence it, but noticed the caller ID. I was shocked to see the name flashing was "Stacey." I had left her in my contacts all those years. It had been over six years since the last time I had heard from her and had listened to her chapter. She then texted, "I need to talk now." So, I called.

She launched right into the conversation with, "Jay, I wanted

23

to tell you what a good life I have now. I'm engaged to a really nice man. He's an accountant. I have spoken about you often to him. Thank you for always encouraging me. I have my own bar now. I bought a bar."

I didn't know what to say. This call was such a stunner and made me feel so good inside. Stacey said, "How are you, Jay?"

I didn't want to bring down the moment. "I'm fine." The doctor appeared in the waiting room as we updated our social media contacts for each other.

I debated about it, but a week later I decided to message her a link to my Facebook page where I had revealed my need for a kidney donor. I heard nothing back from her. Two months later I was in dialysis getting my treatment on a Tuesday afternoon and I got a text from Stacey. It simply read, *"I saw your page. How sad. So sorry. Can I call you?"* I quickly put my headphones on. She asked, "How can I help?"

I said, "I would appreciate your sharing my story."

She interjected, "What does someone have to do to donate a kidney?"

I texted her the link to the kidney donor form from the hospital in case she wanted to learn more about the process. I also gave her the telephone number of a kidney donor named Brian who had offered to share his personal experience about the donation process with any potential donors.

At the end of that summer, I felt well enough to take my daughter and her friend to a baseball game. We are New York Mets fans, but my friend, who works in the locker room at Yankee Stadium, offered me tickets. This was our first game in four years as I had been too ill prior. I had energy that day. That same morning, Stacey unexpectedly called and left a message. "I spoke to Brian last night and then called the transplant center. I am planning to go for my blood test today before I go to the gym." I was blown away.

Just then, I received a text from my friend Scott who had originally put me in touch with Brian. Neither Scott nor Brian knew that I was going to the Yankee game that night. Scott texted, *"Brian is throwing out the first pitch at Yankee Stadium tonight."* I immediately texted Brian that we would be at the game, and we planned to meet for the first time in person after the third inning behind home plate.

As we were getting ready to leave for our journey from Pennsylvania to the Bronx, I received a text from Stacey. It said, *"Got my blood test."* There was a photo of a band-aid on her arm. I was blown away. Stacey called me a few minutes later. Before she could say anything, I said, "Thank you so much. I am taking my daughter to the Yankee game tonight. Brian is throwing out the first pitch. Can you believe it?"

She said, "I went to church this morning and lit a candle and asked God for a sign about whether or not I should donate my kidney. That's the sign! My fiancée and I will meet you at the game."

I was so nervous and excited to see Stacey again after all those years. There she was with her Yankee cap and T-shirt. I shook hands with her fiancé, and Stacey and I embraced as we both teared up. She came around and sat next to me on my left so that I was in the middle with her fiancé on my right. We were together again after all those years and talked like old times.

I looked up at the jumbotron screen above the outfield seats as Brian threw out the first pitch. I then texted my friend Jeff in the locker room. *"Can you meet us after the third inning behind home plate?"*

During the third inning we left our seats. I was dizzy and overheated but we made our way through the stadium to meet Brian. He spoke with us for nearly an hour behind home plate. He even lifted his shirt up and showed everyone his tiny scars from his kidney donation. Brian remarked about the positive energy of the people who supported me. He also whispered something in my ear. "Jay,

I am also O positive like you. If I had known you two years ago, I would have donated right to you."

Jeff arrived from the locker room in the nick of time to meet us. He spontaneously shared with everyone that his father had also been on dialysis but passed away while he waited for a kidney donor two years earlier.

Stacey took it all in. She walked over to me and whispered in my ear. "The only friggin' thing more that could possibly happen would be to catch a foul ball."

We took some photos together and before Jeff departed back to the locker room, he reached in a bag and pulled out two baseballs that had been discarded from that night's game. He handed one to Stacey and one to my daughter, who quickly gave it to her best friend. We ate dinner at the Hard Rock Cafe inside the stadium after the sixth inning. We talked and talked so by the time we left the stadium the game had been over for two hours.

I was drained. My daughter and her friend took me by the hand and guided me back to the parking lot. The friend turned to me and said, "Jay, your life is like a movie."

Joe's Last Performance

Dialysis was like a big circle of chairs surrounding a large island or nurses' station. The people closest to you became your world in a way. You experienced their pain and discomfort, their ups and downs, and the rhythms of their life as they shared them. I sat in the farthest corner facing the entrance. I could see the comings and goings of patients and staff. My nearest neighbor was just in front and to the right of me and in my immediate sight line. His name was Joe and he was in his late sixties, a right leg amputee, and a somewhat cantankerous person at times.

Joe was upset because he wanted an earlier treatment time. Apparently, an earlier start time would be more conducive to his meal schedule and better for his troubled stomach. Instead of talking it through with the nurse manager he would just start yelling about it from his dialysis chair. These outbursts went on for quite some time.

However, I discovered another side to Joe and spoke to him during some of his quieter moments. He went into great detail about his having been a guitarist in a notable local rock band for many years. He said he had a video of his band's last gig at the Musikfest in Bethlehem, PA, which I had learned was the biggest music festival on the East Coast. I was eager to see the video, and it was clear that Joe was excited to let the staff and patients in the center know that he'd had a life before dialysis and that he was proud to show what he was capable of doing.

Each patient had their own television screen on the wall in front of their dialysis chair. The dietician showed some educational videos from time to time, so I figured it would be easy for Joe to show his last gig to those who wanted to see it. Joe loved the idea and asked the charge nurse if he could bring his DVD in that next Saturday. The nurse was all for it, and Joe's excitement was palpable as we approached the weekend.

Joe came in a bit early that Saturday and presented the DVD to the nurse. She immediately told him that it would not be happening. It was in fact, she said, "against the rules." So why had she told him to bring it in? Joe was devastated. It was as if he was being robbed of the opportunity to show everyone that he had a talent and that he was not just a sick man dependent upon a machine to keep him alive. It was humiliating. I felt so bad for him and I immediately asked Joe if I could take the video home with me so that I could enjoy it.

When I returned to the center for my next treatment, I made sure to loudly praise and acknowledge Joe's musicianship. I could tell that it made him feel good. We exchanged phone numbers and talked about possibly getting together one day. Joe was in the process of being fitted for a prosthesis for his left leg and said he looked forward to being able to drive again. I called him a couple of times that spring, but Joe was not very motivated to get together. His wife would drop him off at dialysis and he usually grumbled as he transferred to a wheelchair on his way inside the center.

I waited in the lobby to be called in for my treatment this one day in late spring, and Joe walked in on his own. He had a new confidence about him with his new leg. Joe then switched his treatment days so that he could have the weekends to go fishing again. I was happy for him and wished him well.

I received a surprise call from Joe a few months later in July. He was very upbeat and said, "Jay, I want to come to your home this weekend and play some music for you."

I was taken aback and thought there would not be enough time to invite some friends and provide him with a proper audience. I said, "Joe, I don't think I can be ready on such short notice. Can we do it another time?"

Joe was insistent. "This Sunday is going to be a cooler day," he said. "The heat is going to break. It is the perfect day. This is just for your family. That is the only audience I need. Please just set up a tent on your back patio so I can be out of the sun and I will just need some help getting my equipment out of my car." I agreed and asked if there was anything special that he would like for lunch. Joe specifically asked for a hamburger and macaroni salad. My daughter and I purchased a canopy tent at a local sporting goods store and my wife agreed to the lunch menu.

That Sunday was a beautiful sunny day and a bit cooler as predicted. Joe arrived right on time by himself. We expected a simple acoustic guitar performance so we were a little surprised when Joe popped the trunk of his car and directed us to unload multiple speakers, a monitor, patch cords, microphones, an amplifier, a mixing board, guitar picks, a music stand, and a stool. Joe was wearing a blue bandana tied around his forehead, a white T-shirt, and black shorts with a green neon strip up the side.

It took him about forty-five minutes to set up under the tent. He was ready to rock and he played everything from Led Zeppelin to the Beatles to Pink Floyd on his electric guitar including "Whole Lotta Love," "Day Tripper," and "Wish You Were Here." Joe sang fervently in a passionate raspy voice. The music blasted throughout the neighborhood. The first set lasted about an hour, and then we sat under our umbrella table for lunch. Joe loved the hamburger and he especially enjoyed the macaroni salad. Joe turned to me after lunch and said, "I would like to play one last set." He jammed for about forty more minutes.

My daughter and I carried all of the equipment back to his car. We thanked him for a great performance. Joe drove off looking exhausted but satisfied.

When I went back into dialysis the following Tuesday, the staff told me that all Joe had talked about was his concert at Jay's house. He raved to them about the experience, the feelings that he had playing one more time, and of course about the macaroni salad.

A few weeks later at the end of my treatment, I sat alone in my chair waiting to be cleared to go home that night. I was usually the last patient there. The nurse approached me and told me that she had some bad news. I was confused and worried. She said, "Joe passed away this morning at 5:00 a.m. I know how much you cared about him and just wanted you to know." I started crying uncontrollably. The nurse held my hand tightly, and when I caught my breath she said to me, "Aren't you glad that you were part of making Joe's last performance possible."

Mom Came Alive

When I was thirteen years old, in the fall of 1983, my mother was working on revising her dissertation for her doctorate at Teacher's College ("TC"), Columbia University. That spring, she planned on defending her dissertation to become Dr. Gittleson. She was already a part-time English professor in downtown Manhattan at the Fashion Institute of Technology. One evening, we ate dinner together as a family in the TC cafeteria right across the street from our apartment building. My brother, father, and I remained there for dessert as my mom headed up the long block to the 116th Street subway station next to the main gates of Columbia University to get to her teaching job.

About thirty minutes or so later, a police officer approached our dining table and informed us that my mother had been mugged by two men just as she was about to go down the subway steps and had been taken to a nearby hospital. Apparently, my mom had been confronted by two men, one on each side of her, who demanded that she hand over her purse. While one guy took off with it, the other man pushed her headfirst down the subway stairs. She tumbled down eighteen concrete stairs until she hit the first landing. In shock, she screamed so loudly that campus police spotted the attackers as they ran away and gave chase. They recovered her purse in the bushes, but only one of the attackers was apprehended.

My mother's head injuries were severe and it seemed like in some ways I had lost my mom as I had known her just an hour earlier. She took a leave of absence from her doctoral work and left us for a few months to be with her family in New Orleans. I was unsure what would come next without her around.

I had looked forward to having a bar mitzvah that year but it was forgotten. When my mother returned home to New York City, I reminded her. She called our dear Rabbi Schwab, or "The Rabbi" as we referred to him, who lived in Lexington, Kentucky. My parents had met him at a temple there where my brother and I were born because my father's first teaching position was at the University of Kentucky.

The rabbi was blind and an amputee with a prosthetic leg due to his diabetes. Amazingly, he traveled to New York a month later in December 1983. He tutored me the best he could beforehand and then presided over my bar mitzvah at a Catskill, New York resort. The rabbi was my hero and role model. Just months after my grandparents and uncle passed away the following year in 1984, my mother put me on the phone with him for a final goodbye before he passed away. He whispered to me, "I love you, Jay."

* * *

My mother had multiple falls over the years at her apartment in New York City after I got married and started a family. These episodes usually occurred after her male companion, Harry, who lived nearby, would get frustrated with her inability to keep up with him and his desire to be more active and go places. They had met at the last remaining local temple in that upper Manhattan neighborhood with its twelve remaining members who assembled for Friday night

Shabbat services in a rented room in the basement of a church located a few blocks from where my mother lived.

My mother had a bad knee and was less and less available for dinners and outings with her "life partner," as she referred to him. It seemed like an on-again, off-again relationship. However, Harry re-emerged in my mother's life in the early days of 2012 when my mother decided to stay permanently at an assisted-living, nursing and rehabilitation facility. They enjoyed nightly dinners and conversation there.

I called one day to speak to my mother at the nursing home and was informed that she was not there. A nurse told me, "She was transported to a hospital downtown for an evaluation." I was confused and concerned. My wife and I drove into the city on a snowy night to find my mother in a hospital not far from where she had done her doctoral work when I was a kid near Columbia University. The medical director was uncertain as to what exactly had caused her sudden and dramatic decline. My mom was transported back to her nursing home but was no longer herself after that. The whole episode led to what seemed like a permanent downturn. Harry, who had become verbally abusive to the staff, was only allowed supervised visits.

My visits to see my mom were frustrating in that she was less and less able to focus on meaningful conversation and sometimes she just stared off into the distance. She also had trouble hearing, and it seemed that her hearing aids no longer worked. After I became acutely ill and near-complete kidney failure in 2015, it was not possible to make the two-hour trip back to New York City to see her. I was fighting for my life.

* * *

Once I started dialysis, I asked a social worker to reach out to my mother's nursing home to let them know of my situation. I so much wanted my mother to be able to understand what was happening with me. I thought about how similar our outgoing personalities were. She and I both loved to get to know people. In some ways, I had followed in my mother's footsteps in becoming an English as a Second Language teacher because I had loved the memories of meeting her adoring foreign students growing up.

We had other things in common like being able to recognize famous people on a subway or on the streets of New York City. One day we sat on a bench in Central Park and she turned to me and said "There's Paul Simon" as he pushed his child in a stroller. Another time in the theater district I spotted my teen crush, Molly Ringwald, leaning against a building. My mother approached Molly and had a fifteen-minute conversation with her while I stood frozen on the sidewalk despite Molly's repeated waves to come over to talk.

When I was in college, we went to see the Pablo Picasso retrospective exhibit at the Museum of Modern Art. As we walked to lunch on a crowded 57th Street, my mother casually said, "That was Picasso's daughter Paloma and her husband." I ran ahead and caught up to them and said, "Is there any way you can wait to say a quick hi to my mom? We were just at your dad's exhibit at MOMA." My mother was still a half block away, walking as fast as she could. Paloma and her husband waited patiently and I made small talk with them until my mother reached us. My mom and I were quite the celebrity spotters.

* * *

One afternoon during my dialysis treatment in August 2017, I received a call on my cell phone from a number that I did not recognize. It looked like a New York City area code and I let it go to voicemail. When I listened to the message, a strange sense of disbelief came over me. I was astounded to hear the voice of my mother on the message. "Jay, this is your mother. When are you coming to visit? How are Ellen and Lizzie doing? Please give me a call back at the nurses' station. I want to talk. Love you." I was in shock and could not believe it. I was blown away as I had not received a phone call from her in almost five years after her downturn at the nursing home.

I missed those conversations and those calls. She was still a typical Jewish mother who was interested in her son's life and family. Many birthdays had gone by without a call. She knew nothing of my kidney failure, which had led to my own parallel decline in health over the same time period.

I called the nursing home and was connected to the nurse on her floor, who said, "Your mother is right here. She has been expecting your call." It felt so smooth and like a dream. My blood was pumping through the dialysis machine as my mom said, "Hi, is this my son Jay Jay? It's so good to hear your voice. When are you coming to see me, bubbaleh?" She sounded so clear. How did she make such a sudden turn for the better? I dialed my wife's number quickly and connected her on a three-way call so that she could hear my mother's voice. "You are not going to believe this. My mom came alive."

Two days later I drove to the nursing home. When I arrived, I asked the supervisor if he could ask Harry to give me some time to see my mother. I had previously learned that Harry was at the home visiting from morning until evening every day afer his visiting privileges were fully reinstated. The supervisor said, "That won't be an issue, Mr. Gittleson." I studied his face. It seemed like he was hiding something. I said, "What do you mean? What happened to Harry?" His head bowed and he whispered, "Harry passed away two weeks ago."

I wondered how she could come back to life in just two weeks since Harry was gone. As I approached her room, the daughter of the patient across the hall from my mother ran up to me. She said, "I was here almost every night and something strange was going on in your mom's room with Harry. He would pull the curtain and not allow your mom to leave the room so that she could eat in the dining room. He only fed her food that he brought in. I think he was poisoning her."

I was shocked and asked the management some questions. They related to me that when Harry was diagnosed with cancer, he had informed them he had bought a burial plot for her next to his in a Jewish cemetery. I did not know he was dying of cancer nor did he know I had end-stage renal failure. The woman across the hall remarked that she overheard Harry say, "I want to be with Sandy forever." She added, "I had my suspicions about Harry. It was just a gut feeling."

I did not know for sure exactly what had happened all those years since her downturn. All I knew was that my mom was back.

When I entered her room at the nursing home, my mother noticed the blue rubber bracelet on my right wrist and the long, raised bump protruding up my arm.

She said, "Why are you wearing that?" I said, "Mom, I am on dialysis. I need a kidney transplant." Her face looked surprised and concerned. "I wear the bracelet because I have a fistula, which is my lifeline access for treatment. The bracelet is a reminder that I can't get blood pressure checks or blood draws on that arm."

My mother reached over to touch my wrist and felt the vibration and pulsation of the blood flow rushing through my arm. "Can you get another one? I want to wear it."

I took off the rubber bracelet and placed it on her left wrist. My mom said, "I will not take it off until you get a transplant."

The Best There Is

My mother joined a twelve-step group when I was a kid. She lost a lot of weight and became an active member. I remembered that she had made a lot of close friends from being in the program and socialized with some of them.

Years later, when she moved back to New York City, she reconnected with the program and with a few of her old friends. A man named Calvin hosted a meeting downtown and was close to my mom. I met him a few times. Calvin was a black man in his early sixties. He had a soft-spoken teddy bear quality and a spiritual presence. Calvin's trademark was his flat tweed hat. He had a big job for a large construction company as a highly paid heavy equipment operator. When he had time off, he took long motorcycle trips across the country with his buddies. He had many years of abstinence in the program, sponsored numerous members, and did outreach in the community.

Calvin had managed to deal with his own issues and had evolved into a person who was all about helping others. Since my mother attended some of the same meetings, they went out afterward for coffee from time to time. After I went off to college, Calvin would ask about how I was doing and my mother would give him updates.

In 1996, I was teaching at a public school in upper Manhattan.

I had a feeling that I wanted to talk to Calvin and maybe ask him for guidance or life advice. I knew that he had many years in the twelve-step program and had helped and sponsored a multitude of people. Calvin was not the type of person to give you empty advice. I sensed that he would rather take you under his wing, guide you, and show you the way to the answer.

I asked my mother for his number and gave him a call. I told him, "I have always been searching for what I really want to do and be in life. I never feel settled."

He said, "My philosophy is rooted in changing from the inside out."

Calvin told me about some of the volunteer work that he was involved in and how it had changed his life for the better. He said, "Jay, I have spent my Monday nights the past twenty years running a twelve-step addiction recovery program meeting at a women's prison in lower Manhattan."

Surprisingly, he said, "In two weeks I want you to come to meet the women. I want you to share your story. I will speak to the warden and get you cleared."

I had not expected such an invitation, but I felt honored in a way and said, "Okay, Calvin."

He seemed happy with my response and quickly said, "I will see you then and never forget—you're the best there is!" That was Calvin's motto and he repeated it often with conviction and encouraged others to say it to themselves and believe in it.

When Calvin picked me up to drive to the meeting, I started to get nervous. "What should I tell them?" I asked.

He said, "Just share your story. Be yourself. If you are real with them, they will receive you well."

My heart was beating fast as we were buzzed through the front entrance and told to show our IDs. Then we went through the metal detectors to get to the main office. Of course, everyone there knew

Calvin, but they were a little puzzled by my presence. We were cleared in and received our visitors' badges and escorted down a long hallway into the meeting room. Calvin took out various laminated signs and placed them all around the table like, "Live and Let Go" and "One Day at a Time."

A loud bell rang and then within a few minutes the women started to come in. They wore green prison garb and seemed puzzled as to who the outsider was at the head of the table. Some smiled at me while others looked me up and down, trying to size me up.

People took turns reading from a paper with each of the twelve steps. As they went around the room, each woman said their first name followed by their addiction. Some women announced that they were recovering alcoholics or drug addicts. Some of them just said, "Addict."

Calvin said, "I brought along a friend whom I thought you would enjoy meeting. Today's topic is 'Attitude of Gratitude.' Jay is going to share first." I was trying to quickly figure out how my story was relevant. My mind was spinning. I heard what Calvin had told me earlier. "Be real with them." I glanced around the conference table and saw curious, expectant faces ready to receive my message. I decided to open up in that moment and go to a place emotionally that I had not gone before.

"I am a teacher at a school uptown. There is a hospital located just a couple blocks from my school. When I walk outside and up the block on my lunch break, I sometimes stare at a third-floor window in that building with an attitude of gratitude. I know what it's like to be locked up. Let me tell you why.

"Six years ago, I was a patient in that hospital and stayed for quite some time in that room that I mentioned. I could not leave and was very scared. Both of my parents were very educated college professors, so it did not have to be this way. No one wanted me. A bizarre set of events ended with my being confined to a psychiatric unit there. I had committed no crime, nor threatened to hurt anyone or myself. I had never even smoked a cigarette or drank a beer in my life. I was a straight-A student.

"A few days into my stay there on the third floor, a patient threatened to kill me after I asked him his name. When I ran down the hallway yelling for help, I was escorted into the day room. Officers arrived and I was forced to drink a cup of orange juice laced with strong drugs. When I had refused it, one of the officers threw me to the ground and pinned my arm behind my back until I submitted. Just then, I saw that threatening patient out of the corner of my eye stroll by in the hallway pointing and laughing at me. I was allergic to the drugs they gave me which was reason to hold me in that third-story room.

"When I was weaned off these medications, I was told, 'We can't discharge you to the street. Your mother won't take you back home.' The hospital staff became my family. The psychologist helped me apply to get into a group home while I was waiting to go to college and I was finally released. A few months later I started college, finished my degree, and graduated with honors in four years, then my master's degree in teaching, and found a job across the street from that hospital all in a six-year timespan."

I was crying a bit and I think my being vulnerable struck a chord with my audience. Throughout my "share" I noticed one of the women to my right was very focused on me. Her big green eyes were generously trained on me with support and compassion. It was quite noticeable. She had shoulder-length, dark brown, wavy hair. Her face was fair and unblemished with full red lips. The green prison shirt she wore sagged a little to reveal a white T-shirt underneath and a small amount of cleavage.

When I finished speaking, everything was a blur to me for a few minutes as each inmate shared on the topic. At the end of the meeting, some of the women asked the guard in the room if it was okay to approach me. I received many hugs and words of encouragement.

One woman said, "Keep up the good work, Jay."

Another woman holding a Bible said, "You inspired us tonight. God bless you."

A very tall woman approached me and said, "Thank you for sharing. Good Luck."

An extremely weathered-looking woman around sixty-five years old, with a jagged scar on her cheek, said, "I am near the end of my sentence. I appreciated hearing from you." I later found out on the ride home that she had done twenty-five years for murder.

The last person to greet me was that green-eyed woman. "My name is Jennifer. I want you to know how much I was moved by your share tonight." Her hug was a little longer and tighter than the others.

I felt energized after this experience at the prison. It made me feel special in some way. Maybe that is what Calvin had in mind when he invited me.

In the weeks that followed, I received periodic calls from Calvin. He told me, "After your visit, the women from the prison group were asking, 'How is Jay doing?' Now they are asking, 'When are you bringing Jay back to see us?' I am getting a little bit worn down by their requests."

He had told me that normally he only had a guest speaker come once and that was it. Apparently, he was getting some pressure from one of the women who was about to be released. She wanted to see me before then.

Calvin called again and asked, "Would you come back just this one more time?"

I said, "Yes, I look forward to it."

My second visit to the prison was right before Christmas. I felt like maybe I was supposed to be part of a celebration for the woman getting paroled. It turned out to be the older lady who had served her twenty-five years who was being released. Most of the other ladies in the room seemed genuinely happy for her. The topic for the meeting was "Making Amends."

I listened carefully to each person as they spoke. One woman spoke about how she wanted to make amends to her kids for being absent in their lives during her incarceration. Each share was heartfelt.

I noticed that green-eyed Jennifer seemed preoccupied during the meeting. She even tried not to make eye contact this time. At the end of the meeting, I received many thanks for coming and more hugs. As I was getting my coat, I noticed as Jennifer whispered something in Calvin's ear and then handed a paper to him. When Calvin dropped me off at my apartment, he handed me that piece of paper. It was her name, inmate number and prison address. I asked Calvin if it was okay for me to write to her. He said, "It's up to your conscience."

I decided to write a letter to Jennifer. A week later I received a two-page letter back with her photo taken at the prison. We started to write back and forth to each other. Eventually, she asked if I would visit her.

One Sunday, I took the subway downtown with a bag of snacks that Jennifer had requested. I got a strange look from one of the guards who had been at the twelve-step meeting and saw a couple of the other group attendees. I waited at a small table in a large room full of people waiting to see their mom, daughter, niece, and maybe girlfriend. My stomach was churning. Was this all a mistake? Just then, a door buzzed and out walked Jennifer smiling from ear to ear. When she reached my table she whispered, "We can't hug, but we can hold hands." I tentatively inched my hand toward hers and she took my hand and weaved her fingers through mine. She told me that when the bell rang in thirty minutes, she would have to get up right away and leave to go back to her cell. Jennifer informed me that a closed mouth kiss on the lips was allowed if we stayed seated at our respective sides of the table. I felt a tug on my hand, which I guessed was my signal to lean forward for the kiss. She had a lot to say. "Jay, I will be released in eighteen months. I want to come and live with you." I was stunned and I froze.

Throughout the months that I corresponded with Jennifer, women had suddenly discovered that I existed as a man. It was all new to me. There was a woman who lived in my apartment building who expressed interest in me. She would call me at midnight sometimes and say, "Take a shower and I will be down in fifteen minutes." Then we would just sit on my sofa looking at each other. Was I supposed to make the first move? I also took a woman whom I worked with out on a few dates as well. What was I doing with Jennifer? Was this normal? I heard Calvin's voice in my head: "It's up to your conscience, Jay." What had I done? Had I taken this too far?

I decided to write a letter to Jennifer.

"I am not ready for a commitment. You are a special person to me, but I do not want to lead you on."

She sent back a letter in response.

"Jay, you hurt me so much. I've been crying all day in my cell."

I could see her tears had stained the paper. I felt terrible.

About a week later I received a call from Calvin. He asked me why I had written to Jennifer. I reminded him that I had asked his permission when he gave me the paper from her. "I told you it was up to your conscience, Jay."

I asked Calvin, "How did you know I was corresponding with her?"

He said, "You've created quite a stir at the prison. Word travels fast in that place."

I apologized for anything that I had caused. He hung up the phone.

I wrote an apology letter to Calvin. He never responded back. Why had he given me the paper with her name and contact? Had I failed the "conscience test"?

About a year later, I received a message from my mother that Calvin had died suddenly. Apparently, when he was on vacation, and for the first time in ten years, he had broken his juicing regimen and splurged on a slice of pizza. He choked on the crust, went into cardiac arrest, and died before the ambulance arrived. I was shocked.

I attended his funeral service at his old church in Harlem. Printed on the funeral program under Calvin's name was his motto, "*You're the Best There Is.*" It was an open casket. He had on his motorcycle jacket and his trademark tweed flat hat. I kneeled next to him. I put my hand on his and said, "I am so sorry for what I did to disappoint you. I wish we could have talked. Rest in peace."

I spoke to my mother after the funeral and told her about what had transpired between Calvin and me the year before. To my surprise, she already knew the story. My mother said, "He regretted breaking his own rule about second visits and for taking the paper from the woman and giving it to you in the first place. Calvin shared with me that you shined in that room with the inmates. Jay, he never saw anyone connect with them like you did. I think that he was a little jealous that you took the spotlight from him."

I have used Calvin's motto over the years in acknowledging people who shine in my eyes. I have learned that everyone is the best there is in their own way.

The Doc I Needed

In the summer of 1984, my brother, mother, and I took a trip to New Orleans to visit relatives and for the World's Fair. We had come to understand that my grandmother was ill and had not left her home or gone outside in many years. Long before, she had been diagnosed as being manic-depressive, and she was being medicated by my grandfather, who was a pharmacist still working part-time at the Katz and Besthoff drugstore a few blocks away from their St. Charles Avenue Apartment.

Their apartment was dark and cluttered with an old, reeking smell of cigarettes. The walls were badly stained from the smoke. My grandmother, "Maw-Maw," was extremely overweight and sat all day in the kitchen smoking and watching a small TV set that was propped up on a pile of old newspapers. She looked like a gypsy with her dark, olive-colored skin that drooped over her eyelids and her long, unkempt hair. Her moo-moo dresses were flowery. Her odor was distinct, and when she pulled me in for a hug and kiss, I tried to hold my breath. Her old push-button phone was her friend as she watched her game shows or thumbed through the *Times-Picayune* newspaper.

We were staying Uptown in my Uncle Perry's shotgun house on General Pershing Street for the summer. It was an old, single-story wooden home, one room wide, with the living room at the front of the house, followed by two bedrooms, with the kitchen at the back of the house. These shotgun houses got their name because you could fire a bullet through the front door and it would exit through the back door.

The woman who lived next door told us that she had not seen Perry in a long time. My Uncle Perry was a quiet forty-year-old man with mental problems who was sleeping on an air mattress in my grandparents' living room and too paranoid to stay at his own home. My grandparents had kept up the rent payments with the hope that one day Uncle Perry would get better and return to live there full-time. Perry had been a brilliant chemical engineer who went to Stanford. The only problem was that he had figured out how to make acid in his lab and tripped out one too many times.

Over the years he took several "trips" back to California in search of something. He was haunted by postcards and notes he kept receiving from his former girlfriend, Peggy, who had left him years prior. He could never seem to accept the loss. She couldn't figure out that sending him postcards, notes, and photos from her married life would set him off to a drug-induced trip back to California, which always left him homeless and penniless on the streets of San Francisco.

The latest postcard had arrived just a few weeks before we had come to town. A couple of nights into our visit we got a call at 2:00 a.m. that he had slit his wrists and taken an overdose of sleeping pills. We raced over to my grandparents' place and saw him being loaded into an ambulance. They pumped his stomach and stitched him up and he survived.

At the end of this turbulent summer visiting my grandparents and the World's Fair in New Orleans, it was time to head back to New York City. My brother and I were not sure exactly what the future held for us as my mother was constantly talking about leaving my father and moving back to New Orleans, where she had been raised, to be close to her family. The uncertainty was unsettling.

We left from Uncle Perry's place, and Paw-Paw gave us a wave goodbye as we got in the taxi. I remember looking at him and studying him as we drove away. He looked like Popeye—he really did. He was skinny and still in pretty good shape. He would flex his bicep like Popeye would do. That was the last time I saw him.

After we returned to New York, my mother tried calling but there was no answer. My grandmother always sat in the kitchen by the phone. No answer. After a couple of days my mother became extremely worried and she called her cousin who lived in New Orleans, not far from them. He went over and knocked but no answer so he called the police. The police decided to break down the door. They found my uncle dead in the bedroom slumped on the bed with a gunshot wound to the head. Both of my grandparents were dead lying next to each other in the kitchen. There was a small piece of a brown grocery bag with some dollar amounts on it that said "checking" and "savings." My grandfather had murdered his wife and son before committing suicide. The final bullet had ricocheted off my grandfather's skull and pierced a hole right between my mother's eyes in the family portrait in the living room.

My mother's family was well known in uptown New Orleans. In the 1940s, '50s, and '60s they ran the well-known Herman's Pharmacy, which was the hub of the community. The news of their deaths was front-page news and on every news station. After a triple funeral my father returned to New York. My mother, brother, and I stayed in New Orleans.

Thus began a different and confusing period in my life. My brother acted out his emotional disturbances. He took his racing ten-speed bike out in the middle of the night in New Orleans through bad neighborhoods and we wondered if he would come back in one piece. He was driven to these emotional outbursts in the middle of the night while I stayed frozen and by my mother's side. I thought I was supposed to be strong. I was scared to let out my emotions. I couldn't do it. It was like an emotional paralysis. I froze internally. It was like everything inside of me went silent in a deafening kind of way.

My only solace that summer was watching Dwight "Doc" Gooden pitch on national television while I was down in New Orleans. In the spring of 1984, "Doc" was a nineteen-year-old rookie phenomenon pitcher for the New York Mets. I was a fourteen-year-old attending McBurney School in New York City as Gooden launched his meteoric baseball career. In New Orleans, I set up a color TV set and antenna in the back room of Uncle Perry's place. We would get po-boy sandwiches and Barq's root beer and I would pray that the Mets would be the featured team on the national Game of the Week and hope it was Doc Gooden's turn to pitch. He was must-see viewing so I did see him a few times that summer on TV. I clung to him—to his every pitch—for reassurance.

Gooden's high leg kick tucked under his chin was like my feeling of safety somehow as he struck out batter after batter. I held my breath as he struck out the side in the All-Star Game. He was the youngest ever to do it. Gooden had become known as "Doctor K." K is a strikeout in baseball scoring, and the nickname represented his surgical precision at striking out batters.

I needed to know he was there. I could rely on him to deliver. It was the beginning of the end of innocence for both of us. Doc was thrust into the national media limelight while still in his teens. I was forced to have to deal with the tragic deaths of my grandparents and uncle.

Doc Gooden went on to win the 1984 National League Rookie of the Year Award. The next summer, I went back to New Jersey to visit my father, who was staying in a rented room. I looked forward to the chance to go see the Mets play at Shea Stadium. My father was not too enthusiastic about taking me to a baseball game. When I did convince him to take me to a few Mets games he would study his manuals and textbooks while we sat near the roof in our $5 seats in the upper deck of Shea Stadium. One day in the middle of that summer of 1985 I convinced him to buy scalper seats, which were on the field level. This would enable me to get close to the field during batting practice when the players were warming up.

When we got to our seats I looked toward the field and noticed a couple of Mets players running wind sprints on the warning track. I recognized one of the guys to be Dwight Gooden! I was mesmerized just watching him run back and forth as he did his in-between-starts workout. He would not be pitching that day. I noticed that the ball boy was asking one of the trainers to go out and get Doc to come and take a photo with his parents, who were sitting near the field. I could see it developing and so I started to make my way down the stairs toward the field.

Just as I got down there Doc had jogged in and was posing for the photo. I was so excited to see him in person and up close. I did not even think about an autograph, but what I really wanted was to shake his hand. He started to jog back to the outfield and something came over me. I shouted "Hey, Dwight" really loudly. He stopped and turned around to look and he saw it was me shouting. He smiled and ran back toward me. I couldn't believe it.

He had a big gold tooth in front, and when he smiled it stood out so much to me. Almost like in slow motion he came toward me and stretched his arm out and extended to shake my hand. His huge hand wrapped around mine and he said, "Hey, buddy, how are you?" I never asked for an autograph as I was just amazed he came back to me. The stadium was just filling in with fans at this point and as I turned back around to go back to my seat the usher said, "I know you're not going to wash that hand again." I returned to the seats and my father was busy with his textbook as I was practically hyperventilating.

I shook hands with Doc Gooden during his record-breaking 1985 season, which culminated in his receiving the National League Cy Young Award for most outstanding pitcher. He achieved the triple crown of pitching (most wins, most strikeouts, and best ERA in the NL) while finishing the year with a 24-4 win-loss record, a 1.53 ERA, and 268 strikeouts. It was one of the greatest pitching seasons in Major League history. In 1986, Doc led the Mets to a world championship.

Not long after the championship season, media reports confirmed that Doc had drug and alcohol addictions, and his erratic behavior led to positive drug tests, suspensions, and stints in rehab. I was devastated to see my hero sidelined. I followed every article and news report and hoped that things would turn around for him. He was the Doc I needed.

Who would've thought that thirty years later I would get to meet Dwight Gooden again? I heard that Doc was coming out with his memoir. He was doing a series of book signings around the metropolitan area. It was advertised that he would be signing the book at the Yogi Berra Museum in New Jersey. When I got to the table for Doc to sign my book, I first shook hands with him and told him, "You shook that hand in 1985 and I haven't washed it since." He laughed. I spontaneously thought to ask if Doc could make a video message for my close friend Masa in Tokyo, who had grown up in Japan as a super Mets fan. A quiet, young techie guy, Jim, who was working with me that day, held the phone steady for me as Doc spoke.

We walked to the parking lot and I got in the car, but Jim would not get in for some reason. "Hey, come on," I said. "I want to drive you home before we hit traffic."

He refused to get in the car and said, "I won't get in unless you go back in there and give your business card to Gooden. You should work with him."

I said, "It was a great moment. I don't want to ruin it."

"Well, I'm not getting in the car," he said.

This was all so weird to me. Jim never really initiated any conversation and was normally such a reserved guy. He had such a different, almost spellbound look on his face. His personality had changed in those few moments. I decided to go back in. The director of the museum recognized me from previous events I had attended and said, "Sure Jay, you can go back in."

As I was entering the auditorium, I bumped into a man in the hallway as I was holding Doc's memoir. The man said, "Don't you want me to sign that too?" It was the author, Ellis Henican, who had written the book with Doc. He had his hand extended so just to be polite I went along with it and he signed the book. Apparently, Ellis had several bestsellers co-authored with famous people from various walks of life. Ellis asked me what I did and I told him I worked with motivational speakers. He said, "You seem like a nice guy. Maybe you want to work with us. We will be doing some speaking engagements with the book." I was a little surprised and titillated. Ellis told me to contact Doc's agent, Ron Goldstein. I copied the number down from his phone and told him it was great meeting him. I saw my young techie friend Jim out of the corner of my eye nodding his head in approval. He didn't say much as usual on the way home.

A few days later I decided to call the agent just for the hell of it. I couldn't imagine working with my childhood sports hero or how that conversation would go. We kind of hit it off on the phone. He said he would talk to Doc and get back to me to see if he was interested in working together. A couple of days later I got a phone call from Ron and he said that Doc would like to work with me.

I was very nervous being thrust into the role of Doc's personal manager at certain events, but I have to say that I enjoyed it and just went with it. It was a thrill directing and taking care of Dwight

Gooden sometimes. I really felt like it was what I was supposed to be doing. I got to talk to the author Ellis one day at an event and he told me that his family was from New Orleans too. He had grown up there. He told me that the best memories of his childhood were hanging out with friends after school at Herman's Pharmacy playing pinball right next door to his family home! I was dumbstruck. I said, "Do you remember Herman the pharmacist and his wife at the cash register and the pretty teenaged girl scooping ice cream at the soda fountain?"

Ellis said, "Of course I do."

I said, "They were my grandparents and my mother!" Ellis was floored.

I organized speaking events for Doc that included a 2014 school program to be used as part of a documentary for the sports network. It took place on May 14, which was the anniversary of his one career Major League no-hitter eighteen years earlier. Doc reminded me of how emotional he was that day, then pitching for the New York Yankees, as his father was very sick in the hospital. He pitched what would be the last game his father would ever see before passing away. His father had been on dialysis for twelve years. That night, my daughter and I were his guests at Citi Field for the Mets-Yankees subway series game with box seats right near the field.

I invited Doc to have dinner with me and some friends while on dialysis in 2018. On the way home, he leaned forward from the back seat as I was driving and said, "We were meant to meet and be a part of each other's lives. I know what you're going through is hard. You're a good man, Jay." We connect on that level. Decades after watching my childhood hero on TV during his glory days, Doc is still there for me.

The Perfect Life

I was unsure of what the future held for me as I prepared to start dialysis in 2017. I thought about calling a person named Mickey Bott, who had made a very positive impact on my life. I had met her as a tenth-grade student in 1985 at a private school that I attended for one year in New Orleans called Metairie Park Country Day. Mickey was a guidance counselor there who was a unique, outside-of-the-box type of person. Mickey had a quiet confidence and a sensitive ear. Her kind, gentle face was an invitation to be in her presence. In her fifties, she had piercing blue eyes, shoulder-length, salt-and-pepper hair, a fair complexion, and rosy cheeks. Mickey was cool and related so well with her students.

Mickey taught a class that was mandatory for all students. The curriculum was based on Effective Human Interaction Techniques (EHIT). I remember Mickey telling us that the idea for such a class came from a privileged, hotshot stockbroker who had been in a near-fatal car accident. When he awakened in the hospital from a coma with numerous broken bones, he somehow had an epiphany that he had not been a very good person. Prior to the accident he'd thought he had the perfect life, but he now decided that he wanted to write a curriculum that taught young adults about becoming better people. It was a good program for this school of rich kids who were all about money and status, but who were perhaps maladjusted in other areas. Many of them drove to school in Porsches or BMWs but had anxiety, depression, or substance abuse issues.

We all had a journal in class in which we would write to Mickey about certain topics each week, and then she would write back to each student. One time she wrote back telling me how well-liked I was but I did not believe her. As an overweight kid who had experienced major family tragedy and loss the year before, I did not really feel that I fit in at that school. However, I knew that Mickey saw me and heard me. Even though we did not have too much personal contact, other than through those journal entries, her presence made me feel a degree of safety and comfort at that school. I was living with my mother and older brother in a townhouse in New Orleans and I finally felt more settled at home and in school.

* * *

After the tenth grade, I never did make it back to my New Orleans home and the private school after a summer visit to see my father in New Jersey.

I lost contact with Mickey until twenty-five years later in 2010. By chance I met a woman at a conference in New York City who was from New Orleans. After I mentioned that I had attended that private school her demeanor changed. She had also gone to that school and as it turned out she had been Mickey's next-door neighbor growing up and was friends with one of her sons. She later messaged me Mickey's cell number.

I wondered if Mickey would even remember me. I left her a voicemail and thanked her for how the seeds that she had planted long ago influenced what I was doing in life. Mickey called me back and told me that of course she remembered me and my message was one of the most meaningful of her entire career. She also invited me to come back to New Orleans and spend a whole day with her. Mickey had just retired from working at the school the year before at age seventy-five and told me that she had just returned from a cross-country trip with her husband on their matching Yamaha motorcycles! I made reservations but then got busy and canceled the trip. I regretted not returning to see Mickey in 2010.

* * *

I was thinking of Mickey again seven years later as I was about to start dialysis. I still had her number and called. Now eighty-two years old, she told me, "Jay, we will never lose touch again." Her church in New Orleans began to pray for me and we messaged back and forth.

I decided to return to New Orleans to see Mickey on my Reconnection Tour. I arranged a weekend in December 2018 and traveled with my daughter to see her. We left for the airport right after my dialysis treatment on a Saturday evening and planned to return two days later in time for my next dialysis session.

Lizzie met Mickey for the first time at about the same age that I had met her all those years ago at the school. We also met her husband, Fritz, also in his 80s, and were invited to stay at their beautiful home in Uptown New Orleans. They lived not far from where my mother had grown up above my grandparents' Herman's Pharmacy in the 1940s and '50s. I was not sure if they knew the tragic circumstances of my grandparents' and uncle's deaths in the summer of 1984.

It was late when we arrived at their home that Saturday evening, but I could not hold in my thoughts and stories. I had wondered if Mickey even knew as my guidance counselor in 1985 what had transpired that year before?

Fritz was a prominent aviation lawyer and former war hero

pilot. He was a truly sensitive person and not only listened to my emotional story but cried with me and understood me. Mickey seemed a bit overwhelmed or uncomfortable, and even though she had suggested that we all retire for the evening, I just felt that I had to share my story that I had held for over thirty years.

The next morning, we got up early and Lizzie was eager to see New Orleans for the first time. As we tiptoed down the stairs to the front door so as not to awaken anyone, we noticed a letter left for us wedged in the banister. It read:

Dearest Lizzie (and her Dad),

The way you listened to your Dad warmed my heart. You listened to him intently and so respectfully. That was <u>hugely</u> important. You were not judgmental or feeling sorry for him. You <u>were</u> saddened by his plight—a very young boy having to feel rejected by his whole family—and yet he survived. He has <u>you</u>, who loves him in the strongest of ways—a quiet and complete acceptance. He <u>trusted</u> you (and me) to listen, understand and love him while he told us his deepest feelings. He somehow even knew he could trust Fritz who is the kindest, gentlest person I know, who also understands everything. You are so special—as is your Dad—you two are blessed to have each other. That makes up, I suspect, for much of his pain. We love you both. —Mickey

Lizzie and I rode the St. Charles Avenue streetcar to have breakfast at Camelia Grille. We then rode all the way down to the French Quarter and walked around. I randomly picked out an unusual green, polished, heart-shaped stone at a quaint mineral and gem shop on Royal Street as a token gift for Mickey. We met Mickey and Fritz at a restaurant for a lunch of gumbo and fried seafood. Mickey suggested that we go to see a movie that night called *Green Book*, which had just come out in theatres.

Lizzie and I walked with her to the famous and newly renovated

Prytania Theatre just a few blocks from her home. As we held hands with her, I thought, *This was the day I had waited so many years to spend with Mickey.* During a scene in the movie, one of the characters grabs a green rock that looked very similar to the one we had given to Mickey at lunch. Lizzie and I leaned forward in the darkened theater and looked at each other like "wow" at that coincidence.

The day ended with more conversation in the kitchen. I told Mickey and Fritz about the work I had done booking inspirational speakers who had overcome major adversity and now shared their stories with schools and other organizations. I remarked that Mickey would be an amazing speaker. She said, "Jay, I don't think I would fit in your speakers bureau because I have not overcome any major challenges. I have had the perfect life. All of my dreams have come true."

After returning home, I kept in touch with Mickey through Facebook and texting as I continued my search for a living kidney donor. About eight months later in August 2019 I was shocked to learn that Fritz had passed away suddenly after a brief illness. I reached out to Mickey and she was in a state of shock and grief as the love of her life was gone. She could barely talk or make any sense of it. Just a few months later her daughter died in her sleep from a heart attack. Mickey seemed like a shell of the person whom Lizzie and I had spent the day with less than a year earlier.

My beloved guidance counselor was dealing with major grief and loss at age eighty-five. I wanted to be there for her and wrote to her, "I love you, Mickey. You mean so much to me." She wrote back, "Thank you, dear Jay. I do know you indeed love me. You are among those who understand and can comfort me effortlessly."

A Bad Breakup

It was national news in March 1987 when four teens made a suicide pact in Bergenfield, New Jersey. Their dead bodies were found in an idling car behind the garage door of one of the older teens' apartment complex. I was living in a room behind a store just down the road in the next town over.

I wondered why teens my age with girlfriends and cars would do such a thing. I had no access to a car or a garage to even think about such a plan. My life seemed to have so much less to live for than what those kids were dealing with. I had always loved going to school, never even drank or did drugs. I just wanted a future.

I lay on that mattress on the floor of that room with my twelve-inch Onwa Kuwasha color TV set connected to a long, corded cable TV box. I watched the local news and *Nightline* each night listening to stories of copycat teen suicides all over the country after the "Bergenfield Four."

Just months earlier, after I completed the tenth grade, I had gone back to visit my father for the summer in New Jersey. I had looked forward to seeing my beloved New York Mets play at Shea Stadium that summer. I had grown up in the New York/New Jersey area so it was familiar territory. My father had rented a room behind a store in Teaneck, New Jersey, where he was a professor at Fairleigh Dickinson University.

At the end of that summer, I was ready to go back home to New Orleans, where I lived with my mother and brother. My father informed me that it had been a one-way ticket. I was not aware that my father had not paid the private school tuition and my mother basically did not want my financial burden. Here I was in this room with nowhere else to go. I had thought that I would be there just for the summer while all along my father knew that my mom did not want me and that I would have to live with him. It was shocking and crushing to me. My father, in the process of divorce proceedings with my mother, was already in a new relationship with a Polish woman who worked at the university.

I lay down on the mattress on the floor in the room and protested. I told him I was not going to the local public high school. When my father was threatened by local authorities for not having me in school, a social worker from the school district named Mary Anne reached out to me. She convinced me to come to her office, which was just a few blocks from the room.

Mary Anne was an older, chain-smoking, divorced woman with three teenage kids. She became my only contact with the outside world as I was mostly by myself in that room and saw less and less of my father. He was mostly living with that Polish woman in another town.

Mary Anne always encouraged me to come to her office for talks. Every time I went, she bumped up the time I was there. It started at thirty minutes, then forty-five, then an hour. I ended up spending a lot of time there in her office. She knew my father was not providing for me and would frequently take me for a ride in her old beat-up car and treat me to hamburgers at Burger King. She asked me about going to school and I insisted that I did not want to go. So instead, she started having tutors meet me at her office.

I did not realize it at first, but I was being tested. I thought it was fun because I got to talk to people one-on-one and they gave me IQ tests on different subjects. I was learning French, science, and other subjects. After a few months, she asked me to go to school for one period at the high school. I went to one period and then she asked me to try going for two and then three. Little by little I started ending up at school most of the day. She tricked me into attending and I was on my way to completing the eleventh grade.

I had come to be pretty much on my own. For money, I took a job as an office assistant at a local travel agency and rode my bicycle to get around town. I tried calling my mother in New Orleans, but eventually my father cut off the long-distance phone service in that rented room behind the store. There was an old woman who lived upstairs with her two mentally retarded adult children. They controlled the thermostat for my room. It was very cold during winter in that room. Since I had no control over the thermostat, sometimes it would be freezing and other times it felt like a sauna.

Some months later, I was trying to open a window in the room to get some air. When I went to try and loosen the window by banging on the old wooden window frame, my hand slipped and went through the windowpane. I thought that I needed stitches. The next time I saw my father he was annoyed to have to take me across the street to the hospital emergency room. He accused me of doing this on purpose and insinuated that it might have been a self-inflicted wound. I thought to myself if I wanted to do something like that, I would need a car, a hose, and a garage and it would be so much easier.

One day as I walked back home to the room from the school, I started feeling very weird. I could not feel my legs underneath me. It felt like I was floating. There was a hospital a block away, but instead of going in, I went back to the room and became very disoriented. My anger toward my father and my lonely days and nights by myself in that room had caught up with me. I started to feel very anxious and desperate but I was also very frozen.

As I looked out the window, I saw a snowstorm outside. I was cold and paralyzed with fear and losing touch with or maybe coming to grips with the reality of my life. I lay down in the bathtub with a blanket and started writing my thoughts in a small calendar book that I carried and lost a sense of time as maybe two or three days passed. I made a plan to walk to the nearby hospital but when I looked outside all I could see were huge mounds of snow.

I finally broke from the reality of my situation in the first few days of January 1988 in the cocoon of that room behind the store. I was alone in this breakup, with my mind cycling through alternating feelings of rage and euphoric hopes that indeed the world outside was assembling to rescue me. If only I could wait long enough for help to arrive everything would be okay. I was broadcasting my thoughts to the world and the world was responding through the radio and television. I knew I was not alone. The world knew of my plight and would make it right. I would be on TV soon to be celebrated for making it through this struggle. I already felt the warmth and support of families who would soon see my rescue broadcast live on TV.

If only I could time this right. I would need to navigate the front door. I looked through the peephole and could see that fuzzy, narrow passageway to freedom. I told myself, *Just wait until it stops snowing. Enjoy this time and attention that they are giving you on your favorite shows.* I never missed Letterman. He was there for me, and Ted Koppel would not let me down. It was a waiting game. Eating and drinking never crossed my mind. Sleeping was a thing of the past. It was a twenty-four-hour vigil for my survival. With every bit of my being, I believed that an army of people was waiting for me if I could only make it out the front door past the mailboxes and through the two outer doors, which would release me from my current situation.

In a rage, I toppled over and emptied the drawers of a small wooden dresser where my father had kept some of his clothes. I swung a broomstick violently at the window and repeatedly punched the wall. I saw broken glass on the floor so I put on my Timberland boots and took out the shoelaces so that I would not trip as I escaped. I put on my cherished neon blue fleece jacket and decided to finally make a break for it.

I opened the front door to the room and took my first hesitant steps. I made it to the outer door and all I could see were mounds of snow piled up by snowplows in the parking lot of the hospital across the street. I opened the door expecting to see balloons and banners and TV cameras to document my story. It was the middle of the night. There was no one there. The main road in front of the store was packed down with snow and I could see headlights approaching in the distance.

I stood in the middle of the road waiting for my rescuer. As the car slowly approached and slowed down in front of me, I waved for help. The car did not come to a full stop and the driver nervously peered through the windshield. I jumped on the hood of the car but slid off as the car suddenly pulled away. I tried to open the passenger doors of two more cars but could not get in. I started running up the street right down the middle of the road. I thought that I could make it to the police station just three blocks away.

Then I saw flashing police car lights. I waved frantically for them to stop. Two officers approached me and threw me up against the car and handcuffed me and put me in the back seat. My wrists were in so much pain. I kept repeating "713 Teaneck Road," over and over, and I begged them to loosen the handcuffs. "My father is trying to kill me." It was a short one-block ride to the station.

Lieutenant Greene of the police department immediately recognized me. In my earlier pre-teen years, he had overseen a BMX track in the local park where I had competed with my brother. He told the officer to take off the handcuffs and he left briefly and returned with a kitten and placed it in my lap. It was just the comfort that I needed. The officers drove me across the street to the hospital. I begged the one officer to stay with me as I was sure that my father was going to kill me. I thought I heard my father's voice in the emergency room but I could not see anything as the curtain was draped around the bed. A nurse took my vitals and gave me some orange juice. The nice officer agreed to stay with me for a while until he had to respond to another call.

I remember hearing the voices of an elderly man and woman in the emergency room out of sight behind their curtains. I was convinced that the elderly couple were my grandparents on my mother's side. They had been murdered in their home in New Orleans three years earlier in 1984. Somehow, I felt that they had come back to save me and that their murders had been staged. Everyone was returning to save me now.

I agreed to have my blood drawn by a nurse and was offered a warm bed for the night by staff at the hospital. They assured me that my father would not come near me, and I voluntarily walked to an unlocked unit and signed myself into the floor in the middle of the night. I glanced down in the reception area and saw a table full of magazines as the paperwork was being filled out. I recognized Cindy Crawford's face on the cover of *Mademoiselle*. She was so beautiful and it made me feel that there was a happy, hopeful world outside just waiting for me.

There was no one awake and the lights were dimmed in the hallway. I sat in a TV room by myself as my bed was being prepared. There was a leftover slice of pizza in a box and some small cranberry juice cups, which I downed. I finally felt safe and warm. My body had been tensed up for a long time. I finally had the safety to let go and release the tension.

Suddenly, these waves of pain were shooting down my back. I called for a nurse and begged them to give me something for the pain. After a few minutes the nurse gave me an injection and there was relief. Within fifteen minutes the pain returned and I begged for another shot. I woke up two days later extremely groggy.

Miraculously, my brother had flown back from New Orleans and was at my bedside shaking me and told me that I had five minutes to get dressed and get out of there. He had overheard my father, who was being questioned by social services, give instructions to a hospital administrator to commit me to a state facility. My brother guided me down a back stairwell and into a waiting taxi.

Distant Fathers and Sons

I always had a basketball in my hand growing up. It was my form of relaxation. One day, I found a somewhat dark and dingy basketball court located in a rundown office building on the college campus where my father was a professor. The boards on the floor were loose and creaky, the lights were dim, and there were no windows. It was dank and dusty in there, but I loved it since it was usually all mine. I even knew every spot I could get a good bounce out of. My father was almost never around and I ended up shooting hoops all by myself on this rundown court almost every day.

One day, a tall African-looking guy showed up out of nowhere. He looked to be about six-foot-eight and dunked the ball repeatedly on his side of the court. I noticed he had a purple jersey on. It said "BRIDGEPORT" on the front and "BOL" on the back.

My thoughts raced to what the connection could possibly be between this guy and the Manute Bol whom I had been reading bits and pieces about for the past three years in *Sports Illustrated*. Manute Bol was the seven-foot-seven phenomenon who was the improbable 1985 draft pick of the Washington Bullets and now played in the NBA. I was very curious who this guy with the name "BOL" on his jersey could possibly be since I had read in some articles that just before he joined the NBA, Manute Bol had played for Bridgeport University in Connecticut, and this guy had this Bridgeport jersey on.

In between dunks I approached him and started a conversation. "What team do you play for and where did you get that jersey?" He replied in a deep, thick accent, "Nice to meet you. My name is Akila. I play for FDU. I am from Sudan and Manute Bol is my cousin. He gave me this jersey before he went to NBA." My jaw dropped. I simply couldn't believe it!

I became friends with Akila over the next few months. When a new gym finally opened up at the university, he got a work-study job as a security guard for extra money, checking people's ID cards. I went there almost every day to shoot around and he would let me in without an ID.

One day in the fall of 1987 I was in the gym shooting around when Akila shouted out to me, "Hey, Jay, someone is on the phone here in the office and he wants to speak to you." He was a quiet kind of guy, so I thought it was out of character for him. Akila handed the receiver to me, and as I put it to my ear, I heard a deep voice. "How are you, Jay? I heard you know a lot about me." It was Manute Bol on the line. Apparently, Akila had told Manute what a big fan I was and how much I loved him and knew about him. So Manute said, "I'd like to invite you to come to my basketball game. The Washington Bullets are coming to the Meadowlands in New Jersey to play the New Jersey Nets. So come to the game!"

I thought, *Wow, this is pretty amazing.*

About six weeks later the big day arrived. Our group piled into my father's old Mercury Monarch and drove to the Meadowlands, which also included another African cousin named Paul. Manute had left complimentary tickets for us at the box office. We were delighted that they were courtside seats.

Manute came out onto the court. He was such a smiley, out-going guy, and so tall I couldn't believe my eyes. He was the tallest player in the NBA. One of his teammates, Mugsy Bogues, the shortest player in the NBA at five-foot-three, stood next to him on the court. Manute waved hello while he waited for his turn in the layup line. If it had just ended there, it would have been enough for me.

I had hoped that Manute would sign a basketball for me, so I bought a brand new one and planned to keep it as a memento. I was very disappointed when arena security made me leave the ball in the office for the duration of the game. However, when the game ended, I was in for a big surprise. John Williams, who was a big, muscular forward on the team, came out into the stands with a message for us from Manute. He took Akila back with him to the locker room. The rest of us were instructed to meet up in the lobby where Akila joined us shortly thereafter. He said, "We are going to follow the Bullets team bus back to their hotel." As we arrived, we watched all the players get off the bus. I saw Manute and said, "That's him! That's him!"

We parked the car and entered the lobby. Akila walked over to Manute and pointed back at me. "That's Jay, that's Jay, that's him over there!" He waved me over, and I finally got to meet Manute. Standing in front of Manute was just amazing. He was so unbelievably tall that you had to tilt your head back as if you looked up at a skyscraper! Manute said, "I'd like to invite you to have dinner with me in the restaurant at the Hilton." I was thrilled.

The entire NBA team was there in the restaurant. Manute sat between the tables. His legs were so long that he had to extend them and thus had to eat off the side of the table. I was lucky and sat right across from Manute and amazingly got to ask him all the questions I ever wanted to ask him.

I had hidden my ball under the table and just waited for the right moment to ask Manute if he would sign it for me. Unbelievably, we stayed in the restaurant all night until early morning. We laughed and talked until about 3:00 a.m. Manute just could not believe I was so interested in his life and career and that I knew so many details about him. I asked him about the trainer in New Orleans named Mackie Shilstone who had worked with him during the summer and helped him increase his caloric intake and muscle mass. Manute said, "What are you, some kind of a genius or something? You know a lot about me."

As we spoke, Manute was momentarily distracted by the other players who socialized with what seemed like groupies. These alluring women apparently traveled around with the team. They were trolling the players, throwing around the idea of which players were ready to go upstairs with them. Manute held his hand up and proudly displayed his wedding ring. He laughed and said, "I'm married now. I'm a married man now." Other players would go off with the women. Everything was funny to him and we all just laughed with him. Manute had ordered a big steak and I ordered too, but I was too excited and nervous to actually enjoy or eat much of it.

I thought to myself how remarkable it was to have met Akila as I sat with all these NBA players. At the end of the night, I still had my ball hidden under the table and knew that it was now or never and asked Manute if he would sign the ball for me. I was thrilled when he laughed and said sure! Of course, I saved that cherished ball all these years and I still have it.

I stayed friends with Akila and ended up going to more games with him. Eventually, he ended up playing out his scholarship and graduated. I continued to follow Manute's career. He played for ten years in the NBA, from 1985 to 1995, with the Bullets, Philadelphia 76ers, Golden State Warriors, and Miami Heat. His 3.3 blocks per game rank second in NBA history. He made about $8 million to $10 million during his career.

Remarkably, Manute made sure to send most of this money to his countrymen back home. There was a civil war going on in Sudan, and Manute belonged to the Christians in Southern Sudan who were fighting a war with the Muslims in the North. Manute was involved in different levels of funding the resistance and the people. Tragically, he lost over 250 members of his family in that civil war. He spent all his earnings in support of hundreds of people in his country, so by the end of his career he was basically financially broke. During and after his basketball career he made several trips to his homeland, survived threats by political enemies, recovered from a horrific car accident in the US, and spared no effort to do whatever he could to help his countrymen in Sudan. He had six children with his first African wife but eventually there was a bad breakup. He did marry again.

* * *

A couple of decades passed, and when I turned forty I joined a gym that had a basketball court. One day I was shooting around and met a friendly young guy. We started talking about the NBA and I reminisced with him about having met Manute Bol back in 1987. He froze, his mouth dropped open, and he said, "Wow, I'm friends with Manute Bol's two sons. They live nearby with their mom and sister." I was stunned. I couldn't believe it. The guy went on to say that the eldest son, Madut, had not been on speaking terms with his father for several years and that Manute was now living in Kansas. "Yeah, next time we're in the gym I'll introduce you."

At first, I was thrilled that I might get to meet the son at some point, but then I started thinking that it would be quite weird for me to rave to him about how great his father was, considering his son was estranged from him. So, a few weeks went by and I didn't see the young guy around again. I felt kind of relieved in a way thinking this meeting was never going to happen. Then I would not need to worry about talking about Manute to his son.

But one day I was in the gym doing my usual little shoot-around when I suddenly felt someone tap me on the shoulder. I turned around and it was the young guy! "Hey, you remember me? You know, Manute Bol's son Madut is lifting weights in the weight room."

I paused for a moment and said, "Oh… Well, that's great, but I'm just going to let that one go. You said he didn't have any relationship with his father. It's going to be kind of awkward for me to talk to him about his dad."

He said, "No, you really should meet him." I turned around and Madut was leaning against the gym wall. It was eerie how much he looked like his father, only he was a mere six-foot-nine.

I walked over and told him that I had known some of his relatives and had met his dad many years ago. He told me that he had just won a high school basketball championship with the famous coach Bob Hurley in Jersey City and was considering two college scholarships. We ended up talking for a while. He mentioned that he had not spoken to his dad for a while. I shared that I did not have a relationship with my father and had not seen him in over fifteen years. Madut opened up a bit and started talking about his scholarship offers. I was trying not to talk to him as a father figure even though I was twice his age.

At the end of our talk, I told him, "I have this basketball that your father signed twenty-two years ago. Would you sign the ball?"

He hesitated and then said, "Yeah, I'll sign it. Come to my gym league game tonight."

It was pouring rain that night, and I took my eight-year-old daughter with me to the gym. When we got to the gym, he wasn't there. We waited for a while thinking he might not show up. Finally, he arrived. These kids in the lobby of the gym thought he was somebody famous because I presented the ball to this very tall guy for an autograph. We heard whispers: "Who's that? Who's that?" Before Madut signed the ball he took a long look at his father's signature already on the ball. I asked him not to scribble on the ball. He took the ball and signed it neatly right above his father's name. You could tell that something was going through his mind. He seemed a little bit fazed. Madut accepted a scholarship to Southern University in Louisiana.

After this unexpected meeting, I was spurred on to want to reconnect with Manute Bol with the idea of working with him as a speaker to help him raise money for his Sudan Sunrise foundation. The woman who ran the foundation said that Manute would love to work with me upon his return from the Sudan, where he was working on building the first school in his home village of Turalei. Manute stayed there longer and got sick while helping campaign with a presidential candidate. A few months passed and I did not hear from Manute.

On June 19, 2010, I got a call from my friend Keith who said that he had just heard on ESPN that Manute Bol had passed away. I was shocked. Apparently Manute had a bad reaction to some medication and didn't make it back to the United States in time to get proper medical care. He died of kidney failure a few days after he arrived at the University of Virginia Hospital. It was the day before Father's Day. It hit me hard. He was forty-seven years old and left behind ten children.

I wondered if Madut had the chance to see his father in his dying hours to say goodbye. I thought about my own relationship with my father and had a feeling that my father was still alive. My father's birthday was that week. He would be seventy-three years old.

I called the Sudan Sunrise Foundation the next morning and spoke to my contact. She said, "Well, now you know why he didn't call you back." I related to her my connection to Madut and asked, "Did he get to say goodbye to his father?"

She said, "I am not sure if he got there in time." I hoped that Madut would not have to go the rest of his life with that regret.

The latter part of Manute Bol's life was about reconciliation and healing. He had gone from funding the military resistance in Sudan to helping in a humanitarian way and evolved into a person with a bigger vision. There were even plans to build a mosque in the southern Christian area of Sudan and to build a church in the northern Muslim area.

I decided to email my father. I didn't know exactly where he lived. I wrote, "Couldn't we find some common ground? Why wait until it's too late to reconnect, or to have some sort of a relationship?"

I then emailed Madut a note of condolence and I told him that I had reached out to my father. Madut wrote back almost immediately that he was proud of me and told me to keep him posted. A few hours later I got a brief email from my father. "I would like to meet my granddaughter. I live in Poland and will be passing through your area in a few months on my way to California."

I went to Manute's funeral in Washington, DC at the National Cathedral. I met the woman from the foundation. The speakers included Senator Brownback from Kansas, Robert McFarlane, former National Security advisor, and Rory Sparrow, vice president of NBA player development. There were some beautiful tributes in the *Washington Post*, *Wall Street Journal*, and *New York Times*. He was a giant, but he also had a giant heart.

At the end of the summer, we expected my daughter's return from sleep-away camp. I rushed out to Whole Foods in Paramus, New Jersey to pick out the freshest fruit for a fruit salad. It was extremely crowded and I randomly chose one of the checkout lines. I noticed the young woman cashier's name tag had an unusual-sounding name. "Where are you from?" I asked.

She looked up and said, "Sudan." I told her, "I knew someone from Sudan who recently passed away." She was curious to know who the person was. I told her, "It was a basketball player named Manute Bol." The woman froze and looked at me with tears in her eyes. "He was my father." I looked at her face and recalled the woman in African garb at the funeral who had collapsed at the end of Manute's funeral service. It was her! I didn't know what to say or do. I asked her for her hand and she extended it. I took her hand and repeated, "I'm sorry, I'm so sorry." The people in line were puzzled. I knew in that moment that I was meant to be there with her at exactly that moment.

In the next month, as planned, my father came from Poland to my home with his wife. I showed my father the special basketball and explained the special significance it had. Even in death, Manute was inspiring reconciliation.

Chain Reaction

In 2018 I was finally approved to be on the kidney transplant waiting list at St. Barnabas Hospital in New Jersey. Their monthly newsletter featured an article about a man named Brian Glennon who had altruistically donated his kidney there a year and half earlier. There was a link to a video of the *Today Show* episode that detailed what had transpired. Brian, a stay-at-home dad with four kids, decided that he wanted to give back in this way to express his gratitude for having a great life. He did not know anyone who was sick or needed a kidney. It was just something that he was inspired to do out of the goodness of his heart.

As it turned out, Brian was the perfect match for an anonymous woman in the hospital database and the surgery was a success. It was amazing enough for him to have saved just one life. However, Brian's incredible act of kindness started a kidney donor chain that became the largest at a single hospital in United States history. His recipient's daughter, who had not been a match for her mother, donated her kidney to save another person on the waiting list and from there the donor chain kept going. By the time Brian and his recipient met for the first time on national television on the *Today Show*, the chain consisted of sixty-four people and counting. There were thirty-two donors and thirty-two recipients. On the show that day were sixteen people in the chain. Eight donors and eight recipients were all meeting for the very first time.

Since I was now actively in the process of looking for a living kidney donor, I thought to post the inspirational video on my kidney Facebook page. Just six months earlier I had set up the page after being convinced that no one could help me unless I told people about my condition. Up until that time I had not told many people that my kidneys had failed and that I was on dialysis. The social media page was my first attempt to let people know of my situation. I posted Brian's story and the next day I received a call from my friend Scott, who had seen the post and told me, "I went to high school with Brian Glennon!" Without hesitating, I asked if he could connect me with Brian.

Within twenty-four hours I got a call from Brian and we made an instant connection. What a great guy. I felt so comfortable speaking with him and I asked him for his help. He said, "Anything, Jay, just tell me how I can help." I asked Brian if he would share his donation experience with my friend Phil, who had recently seen my kidney page and had expressed interest in donating his kidney to me.

I had not been in touch with Phil for about ten years, and he had a lot of questions about the kidney donation process. I gave him Brian's telephone number. I had first seen Phil and his first wife, who was a famous super-model, on *Oprah*. They were discussing their book entitled *Morning Has Broken: A Couple's Journey Through Depression*. Phil had suffered from a major depression episode after his daughter Toby was born in 2001. I had met him in 2008 at a speaking event, where he spoke openly about his condition and recovery. We got together for dinner a couple of times, then lost touch until 2018 when Phil saw my Facebook post about my need for a kidney transplant. Phil messaged me with a lot of questions about kidney donation.

I was in dialysis getting my treatment the following Tuesday afternoon when I got a call from Phil, who told me that he had spoken with Brian and that he was one hundred percent committed to donating his kidney to me. I became extremely emotional in my dialysis chair in that open room. I cried on the phone with Phil and I felt this warm blanket of safety and hope envelop me. Phil said that he was ready to start the evaluation process to become a living kidney donor. After initial testing and follow-up meetings with the transplant team, Phil called me in tears. He had been medically disqualified from donating to me. The devastation was felt by both of us, but we had developed this amazing friendship along the way. Phil became one of my biggest donor champions and told me that he would never stop helping until I found a kidney donor.

Gathering of Gratitude

My close friend Ron was about to have major surgery in Florida. I wanted to surprise him and travel to see him beforehand. I am sure that he did not need me to be there but I felt that it was imperative for me to show my support in that way. I called ahead and scheduled to receive my dialysis treatments in Sarasota for the one week that I would be there. In truth, I also needed to take a break from the grind of those dialysis treatments at that center near my home in Pennsylvania.

Yes, I had end-stage renal disease, so I needed those dialysis treatments to literally keep me alive. However, I had also started to lose hope that I would find a kidney donor. I could not imagine being connected to that machine for five to ten more years on the kidney waiting list or what my quality of life would be as time went on. The staff at my dialysis center knew that I was struggling. After a year and a half, it was very hard to get through those long hours of dialysis. Just when I started to recover from one treatment it would be time for the next one. The nurse said, "Jay, you need to take that trip to Florida. It will do you some good."

About six weeks earlier I told my friend about a dream that I had. I imagined inviting all the positive people in my life to get together for lunch to express my gratitude for their love and support.

He said, "You can call it, A Gathering of Gratitude. Why don't you make a list of all the people you want to invite. Pick a date and a place to meet."

So, I did. My guest list quickly grew to seventy-eight people. Many of the invitations went out to people whom I had already met up with on my Reconnection Tour. I booked a banquet room in New Jersey, which was the same place where my daughter had her Sweet Sixteen party just two years earlier. I also asked some of my friends to do various performances and presentations for the event.

My trip to Florida was supposed to be my respite as the Gathering of Gratitude was scheduled for the day after my return home. I knew that it was going to be hot down there so I had to be sure not to overdo it on my fluid intake. My home dialysis center seemed chaotic most of the time, and I wondered what the experience would be like in Florida. The manager of the dialysis center in Sarasota assured me that they would take good care of me. I also thought it would be a good time to start writing my book at the Holiday Inn, which overlooked the white sands of Lido Beach and the Gulf of Mexico.

I called my friend in advance and wished him well on his surgery. He was a bit surprised when I told him that I had a business meeting in the Sarasota area that upcoming week. "Where will you be getting the treatments?" he inquired. I said, "Fruitville Road." That was about a forty-five-minute ride from where he lived. I did not think that my surprise plan would register with him.

I arrived on Sunday and looked forward to some quiet days at the hotel. I soon found out that would be guaranteed. As I drove up to the hotel in my rental car with my windows down, I smelled an overwhelmingly foul odor that did not fit the paradise of my surroundings. The beach seemed empty and there were only a few cars in the hotel parking lot. As I looked out through the lobby at the palm trees swaying in the breeze, it looked more like a ghost town.

It turned out to be a "red tide" in the Gulf of Mexico. That putrid smell was from a harmful algae or "algal bloom" that sometimes affected Florida's western coastline, which turned the normally blue waters to a reddish brown, endangered wildlife, and made it unsafe for people to enter the water. The condition, much like my own, had worsened over the summer of 2018 and had lingered even until my October visit.

I believe I was one of maybe ten people at the hotel, so I enjoyed the heated pool mostly by myself and it was a surprise to run into anyone. A restaurant on the top floor offered a beautiful view of the Gulf. There was only one waitress for only a breakfast serving each day so I got up early to see the sun rise with my eggs and toast.

I was nervous about my first out-of-town dialysis treatment the next day on Monday afternoon. When I arrived at the dialysis center it looked like a day spa with the palm trees outside as I entered the bright-yellow, Art Deco-looking building with its terra cotta roof. A tropical fish tank stood along one wall next to framed avant-garde paintings created by local artists. Within a minute or two of signing in at the reception area, the door swung open. An upbeat, super-fit, and smiling Latino man with perfectly slicked-back hair approached me with a clipboard. He said with a flare, "Mr. Gittleson, my name is Javier. We are ready to start your treatment."

For a moment I felt like I was at a spa. Everything was sparkling clean and organized inside the treatment room. The nurses and technicians, for the most part, looked happy. There was no yelling or screaming. The manager came out after I was seated in my electronic multifunction recliner. She showed me all the features of the chair including a heated built-in massager. It seemed more like I was at The Sharper Image or Brookstone. She said, "Do you have a blanket?" I shook my head no and she motioned to Javier. In a friendly voice she whispered, "Even if it is ninety-five degrees outside, an air-conditioned room and the effects of dialysis still require a blanket."

Javier appeared with a bright neon green tote bag containing a welcome kit, which included a soft, velvety blanket. A chubby African American woman named Jessica gently inserted the needles into my arm and started the treatment. I was relaxed and told her that I was so pleasantly surprised and relieved. Jessica said, "Aren't all your treatments like this back home?" I thought back on the scary experiences of misplaced needles, and trips to the surgeon to check the access or fistula in my arm.

About an hour into my treatment, Jessica walked over and told me that I had a visitor. Although back home that was a usual occurrence, I was baffled and told her it had to be a mistake. She said, "Your brother is here to see you."

"I have not heard from my brother in nearly a decade," I said. Just then, as if being touched by an angel, the friend whom I had traveled so far to see appeared in front of me. It was Ron who came to sit with me. It was the best treatment I ever had. He sat with me for three hours. We talked and laughed and I even spoke to his wife on the phone to verify one of his incredible stories. After my treatment, he took me out for dinner at a great restaurant in an area called St. Armands Circle, which was not far from my hotel.

As we sat in the open-air restaurant, I looked at my friend sitting across from me and felt both drained from dialysis and exhilarated to be with him. We talked about my gratitude luncheon that was just under a week away. I explained that I was going to give a speech in which I would acknowledge each person and why I was grateful for their being in my life. Ron said, "You have to write this speech down. Do not wing it as it is going to be an emotional day for you. Use this week at the hotel to get it all down."

I took Ron's advice and over those next few days I thought about each person and what they meant to me and wrote it all out.

I did venture out in the heat a few times and lost track of my fluid intake as I enjoyed my iced tea lemonades. The red tide had dissipated and a few beachgoers straggled over to dip their toes in the water.

Ron surprised me again and took me out to lunch the day before my final dialysis treatment in Sarasota. Afterwards, we sat in the hotel lobby and I read my gratitude luncheon speech to him. He helped me tweak a few things and I felt confident that it would be well-received. Ron also gave me a bag full of books written by some of the sports stars he had represented over the years. He had inserted an insightful typed letter to me in one of the books that I would not find until two years later.

When I reported for my last treatment the day before I was leaving to fly back home, I was informed by the nursing staff that I had gained too much fluid from all those iced teas. They said it would be too risky to fly back the next day. After all that planning, how would I make it back in time for the Gathering of Gratitude? My only shot was to get an extra dialysis treatment the next morning. If the staff cleared me, then I could leave for the airport to catch my flight. It worked and I was on my way home.

* * *

On the morning of the Gathering of Gratitude I drove from my home in Pennsylvania to New Jersey and picked up my best friend from high school named Jerry. I had recently reconnected with him. When we arrived at the banquet place he saw my typed speech, which I had put down on a table near the microphone. He took a sneak peek to see what I was going to say about him. It read:

Jerry was my only true friend in high school in Teaneck. We lost touch a few times over the years. He saved my life in 1988. I will never forget it. Jerry told me, "Don't you want to see how your life unfolds?"

As each person arrived for the event, fond memories flashed in my mind about each relationship and time period in my life and the uniqueness of each personal connection. My heart was full of joy as I greeted these special people.

I saw my friend Dominic, whom I had met fifteen years earlier when he was a waiter at what became my favorite Japanese restaurant. Dominic was the first person to call me once I announced that I was on the transplant list. Dominic FaceTimed me when I was in the dialysis chair and immediately told me that he wanted to help me. "Jay, I want to donate my kidney to you. I want to save your life." He tried everything but was unable to do so due to a pre-existing medical issue. He touched my heart.

I had planned a program of presentations done by certain friends who had a variety of talents that I felt would bring out the theme of gratitude. I also wanted people to be entertained and engaged after lunch.

After lunch, I was nervous to begin my speech so I first invited my friend Phil up to do his performance and he grabbed his guitar. Before he started, he spoke to everyone about the origin and meaning of his original song, "Show Me the Way," which he had performed and recorded with his identical twin brother, Seth, as the musical duo called The Aronson Twins. He said, "I asked God to somehow show me the way from the darkness into the light.

"So, I wrote this song and I think it's appropriate because although there's so much light around you now, Jay, I'm sure there are very dark times. You are going to get through them and we are all here to illuminate the way."

Phil had a trained voice and sang in a lively high-pitched falsetto.

Hard times ahead. Been there before. Seems like the darkness keeps knockin' at my door.

Keep up the faith. Don't let your guard down. It's never easy when evil comes around.

Reach out with love. Turn this thing around.

What can I do? What can I say?

Let go let God. Take him by the hand. He'll show you the way to be free.

As Phil was singing, he motioned to one side of the room to sing the words, "Show me the way, Show me the Way," alternating with the other side of the room to sing, "Can't do it alone. Can't do it alone."

It was time for my speech. I pulled out my stapled pages from my blazer pocket, and as I nervously approached the microphone, I got my foot tangled up in the cord a bit. At first, I tried to play it off and acted like it was the beginning of a comedy bit. People laughed. I said, "It has been a long time since I have been on stage. So, Ellen thinks I should just read my speech. No worries, it is only forty-one pages long." More laughs. "I am going to read so that it's not a ramble."

Almost two years ago we were in this same room for my daughter Lizzie's Sweet Sixteen party. I was having trouble breathing because the fluid was building up and I was not feeling well. I would soon have to start dialysis, but was not mentally ready for it. I was talking about my daughter Lizzie and how resilient she was and telling the story of her not giving up in her twenty-lap high school swim team race in her freshman year. I later found out that I got the choke sign in the back from my brother-in-law, who thought I was going on too long. All that mattered to me was that I could see my daughter looking at me from across the room and our eyes locked and it meant something to her.

I added spontaneously, "So I didn't invite the brother-in law today." Everyone laughed.

Today I do not want any choke or cut signs. I get a lot of that at the Dialysis Center trying to talk under circumstances that don't allow for such uninterrupted conversations. "Get to the point Jay! What is your point? Can you summarize?" But I do not want this to be about me. That is too obvious. I know this is about me and I love that. I want to acknowledge all the people here today who mean something to me. You are all very special to me.

A few people in the audience laughed at parts of my speech, especially my ad-libs. It took me back to the body rush that I felt when I had performed at New York City comedy clubs in the '90s. I heard a woman cackle in the back of the room and looked up and saw Patty Rosborough, who had traveled a distance to be there. She was my favorite standup comedian, and our friendship started when I booked her for my comedy shows twenty years earlier. When I went to a local comedy club each year to see her perform, it was like we were old friends all over again. She always told people, "Jay put on the best comedy shows," which always made me feel good.

I was fearful of becoming overly emotional so I read a short paragraph that I had written about my wife and daughter. Then I thought it would be the perfect time to call up Lizzie to make her special presentation. She said, "My dad wanted me to make a video that represented everyone who is part of this day. I tried to get as many pictures and videos as possible from people who really and truly care about him."

It was beautifully done with photos of me throughout my adult life and video "hellos" from other close friends who could not be there. My friend Ron gave me a third surprise and sent Lizzie a video. He said, "Hey, my man Jay bird, Ellen, Lizzie. I just wanted to say that I'm sorry I can't be there on Sunday, but I am wishing you all a very special time. I know that it will be one of the most memorable days of your lives. I do feel very blessed that I had the opportunity to see Jay a couple days this week in paradise. I look forward to us being in better health that we can spend more time together in the future. So, I love you. I'm thinking of you always. You're a great person and you are always in my heart. God bless you always."

I did want to have some comic relief, so I asked my old friend Mike "The Clown" to roast me at the event. Mike is a professional clown and comedian with a thriving clown business in New York. He has been a vegan for decades and is a very skinny guy with a big round nose and is bald on top with a trace of graying red hair on the sides. No makeup was needed to transform him into a clown.

In 1996, while I was still teaching at a school in New York City, he invited me to do an open mic standup comedy session in New York City, which ultimately led to my performing at comedy clubs and later producing professional comedy shows. He took my assignment for the roast seriously. When he approached the microphone, I could tell by his quiet demeanor that he had some firecracker lines ready.

He said, "I've known Jay for twenty years and I want to just say that I never really liked you. I want you to know that." People were a little stunned and only one person chuckled. "I was the best man at Jay's wedding because no other man wanted to be. I volunteered." A few more laughs. "Throughout this whole ordeal not once have I heard you complain since you knew you were going to get a kidney transplant. It's because I really don't listen to you when you talk to me. I just wanted you to know that."

More laughs as the audience caught on. "Jay got into standup comedy and never booked me in any of his shows. I really just want to let you know, Jay, I didn't appreciate that. I'm just letting you know that tonight. I really hate you. It's hard to get spots in standup.

You had connections and you knew Doc Gooden. I was a great pitcher, like a high school all-star, and you never introduced me to Doc. You had all these connections and you did nothing for my career…and then you come up here and tell people I was Pickachu. That's what you remember me by? Pickachu? He's not even relevant anymore. Just like I was never relevant because you never introduced me to anyone. Thank you, Jay. I really appreciate it."

Mike was little by little getting streams of laughter. I had finally given him that stage that he had craved all those years ago and he was on a roll. "Jay and I lost contact with each other for about fifteen years, and those were the best fifteen years of my life. They were fantastic, Jay. My career in standup took off and everything went really well for me. Jay and I used to live near other and I was so happy when you moved away to Pennsylvania. It was like the best day of my life. I tried to grow my hair back and it grew a little. I thought that was a good day. But the day you and Ellen moved was the best day. You always invite me up to PA to visit. I really don't want to come. I hate PA. It's the worst state.

"I'll wrap up. Jay, I love you. You've been a really great friend to me and I feel I haven't been a great friend to you. I'm kidding. I really do love you, Jay and Ellen…and Lizzie. You're a very lucky young lady. You have great parents. You have always had this generous heart, Jay, and to me too. I will see you after the operation."

I was trying to feel the moment for which presenter I should call upon next and knew it should be Cornelius. Sixteen years earlier, I was introduced to Cornelius by one of my wife's cousins. He became one of the speakers at my company, A Vision in Motion. He is a former gang member who became a teacher and high school vice principal later in life and an ordained minister. We have traveled together to speak at some unusual places including juvenile and adult prisons, detention centers, schools, and universities. He always made an impact on people in his own unique way. Cornelius became more than a friend. He was like a brother, father, uncle to me. Cornelius prayed with me on the phone and was always there when I needed him.

He stepped up confidently to the microphone and looked over the audience of expectant faces and said, "We are gathered here today and I'm noticing the somberness of the room because of the gratitude of one man."

Cornelius looked over at me and said, "You ain't going nowhere, man. The kidney is already in you. Where I come from and who I preach to, by his stripes you already whole. It's just a matter of time for the physicality part of it to become reality. For right now think healed. Think done. Can somebody give that a hand? I want you to know I've known and been ministering to Jay for the last almost twenty-some years."

I felt the warmth and sincerity of his words and thought back to all the programs and presentations in which I sat in the audience where he introduced me as his agent.

"We in this room need to understand that each day we wake up until the day we won't. So, you blessed to be alive now. A kidney… nah. You're perfect just the way you are. I want everyone to under-stand something today. I'm not gonna take long because I'm not getting a paycheck." People laughed.

"I give humor but I punch you in your spirit. I want you to hear me today. We're not guaranteed tomorrow. We take love for granted. What we need to give this man right now… Everybody, stand up! I'm gonna show you something. I want you to grab the hand of the person with you. I don't care who it is. Grab a hand. Now everybody look at Jay and say, 'I love you. You're healed.'"

Cornelius looked at me in the back of the room and said, "You've been touched by a whole room of love, not just words. You've been touched. You can feel it coming through you right now from all the people that you spoke about today. Always keep one thing in mind.

God put me in your life for a reason. You're the one who's black; I'm white. So, I'm here to tell you, I love you, man, and so does the connection of all this love today.

"I want to end with one thing. I'm here to tell you that when you go to a cemetery, you see the date that you were born and the date that you died. We never talk about the dash in the middle. That's what's gonna tell the world about what you did and what you're doing. We wake up every day until the day you won't, but what are you doing with your dash? What have you done with your dash? You ain't going nowhere. There's no death day for you. The dash ain't finished yet. It's so hard for men to tell another man 'I love you' without somebody thinking something else. I love you from my heart, and that's hard to find from a man that came from the street who would sit in front of a bullet for you.

"I told you this on the phone. I'm gonna tell you one more time. You stay strong. I'm probably the only one that's gonna tell you there's a miracle waiting. There's a miracle waiting, man. We gotta start blessing you with the impossibility of things in this world. Nothing is impossible. Luke 1:37: 'With God nothing is impossible.' Nothing. Until you see that, understand that. This is not sorrow. This is happiness. I love what your daughter did. Gratitude. We're talking about living a long life. I still got to get out to Pennsylvania and get some of that food you're cooking out there. I'm just saying your dash ain't finished. You still got a lot of work to do, man."

Reverse Psychology

I did a series of phone interviews called "Dialing From Dialysis" with various people from my life during treatment sessions from my dialysis chair. My longtime therapist, Dr. Stern, agreed to let me turn the tables on him and ask him a series of questions, which he promised to answer honestly and thoroughly. Dr. Stern was a clinical psychologist, had practiced as an attorney, and was an ordained rabbi. I always said it sounded like he was a setup to a joke. Dr. Stern had just been diagnosed with lung cancer and was ready to talk.

I asked, "What challenges did you face in your life when you were young and in your adult life and how did you overcome the odds?"

Dr. Stern responded, "The challenges I faced were a sense of chronic anxiety and feelings of being the biggest loser in the world, I suppose. I spent a lifetime looking for places, ideas, thoughts, and therapies that would somehow make it go away. In time, I learned to understand fear and anxiety. It didn't go away, but I learned to use it, mostly manage my own, and hopefully be helpful to others. My life itself is made up of different chapters and places and things I did in this search to somehow maximize life, overcome my fears, and find meaning. I almost tried to be, in a sense, a heroic movie star figure like in the kinds of films as a child I idolized growing up in the '40s and '50s."

I asked, "What was your darkest moment? Did you hit rock bottom? And did you ever lose hope?"

Dr. Stern responded, "This seems terribly silly, but one of the darkest moments I remember was going to college and being blackballed into a fraternity I wanted to be in. As a kid, I felt unpopular and unathletic, un-this and un-that. High school was the same. When I went to college, Tulane University in New Orleans, I thought it would all change and then I got blackballed. It seemed like it must be a universal truth perhaps, in a crazy way. Later, I went to law school in the '60s. I was president of my law school class for two years and hoisted on the shoulders of my classmates at graduation. So, in that sense of developing social skills and sensing whatever abilities I had, it was answered. I learned how to deal with people. I learned that the fears I had were within myself and that they weren't external or necessarily true."

I asked, "What was the turning point for you when you knew you were going to make it?"

Dr. Stern responded, "I don't know if today I know I'm going to make it. It's like there's always that fear, but to understand that one has the ability and resources to do so. The question is a very valid one and I'm not sure if I've ever arrived at it. I know I can be effective in communication skills but I'm always shocked that someone pays money for it."

I asked, "Who or what was your inspiration in fighting against the odds and helping you out of the darkness?"

Dr. Stern responded, "My mother had a brother whose name was Abe Newman. He was a very tall, lean, kind-hearted, soft-spoken, lovely, loving human being whom I somehow wanted to model myself after. Whatever the yucky poo or cynicism that the days could bring, there were people like an Uncle Abe. Later, as I got more into Judaism and the perspective of living in Israel and other things, I was fortunate to meet a number of people that were like an Uncle Abe as to character, virtue, and kindness.

I asked, "Did anyone know what you were going through?"

Dr. Stern responded, "I think at a younger age, I thought I was the only one that had anxiety. I thought that somehow, I was plagued by some terrible curse. Eventually, it hit me that the only person that could probably take care of me was going to be me."

I asked, "What could someone have done to help?"

Dr. Stern responded, "Be a good listener. Be kind and loving. I don't know if it's ever enough, but I think we give what we need. One tries to be kind and loving to others, because that's what we ourselves need."

I asked, "Did you think you were going to make it?"

Dr. Stern responded, "I thought if I found the right girl, or the right place, or the right temperature, or found the right something or another, that I would make it. At times, I did find the right girl or the right situation, but it was temporary. Making it for me for many years was finding something that would make the fear go away."

I asked, "What is your biggest challenge today?"

Dr. Stern responded, "Staying alive and being sharp."

I asked, "Did your challenges help you redefine your personal mission statement in life?"

Dr. Stern responded, "The challenges have become a personal mission. Because of my own search, I've been able to at least get some material, perspective, stuff, words, ideas that I can share with others. As I share with others, sometimes I find myself talking to myself. I think we are always struggling as to whether life is just chaos, and nothing, or whether it's meaningful. If it's meaningful, regardless of the pain, it's meaningful."

I asked, "Was there a dream that you never fulfilled?"

Dr. Stern responded, "When I was young, the idea of being cool or popular or whatever, had enormous appeal. I took a lot of acting workshops in Los Angeles, but I did not have the balls to stay with it. I philosophized out of it that your life *is* the greatest story told and that you are the star of your own story—the writer, director, actor. I wondered if it was such a grand thing to try to make a career on winning other people's approval. I remember being in a play, Shakespeare's *Midsummer Night's Dream,* and giving a speech by one of the players, Demetrius. I remember giving it and hundreds of people applauding and it was such a rush. I think it was better than any orgasm I ever had. So, I could understand the appeal. It was like being bathed in a glow of love."

I said, "Great interview. You really opened up, Dr. Stern. I just wanted to ask if you could share your personal experiences with me or any other observations or feedback."

Dr. Stern responded, "Sure. My personal observations are the day I saw you. I loved you because you looked like my stepfather. I just had a feeling for you. It was just your physical look. I think I showed you a picture of him one time. It was just a certain chemistry I felt and your passion, your feelings, your intensity, your effervescence, just all of that drew me. I could also see your fears and your vulnerabilities and what you had gone through and it was always wanting to convince you that you could manage or even get on top of those feelings and fears and the rush and the feeling it's too much.

"I always saw your best in raising your daughter and I still do. I see how she is today. I saw that in A Vision in Motion, your professional product, how good you were. You didn't just book speakers, but you basically became connected, involved, went, and arranged. You threw yourself into life fully. I wanted you to know it.

"It seemed like you always were pushing away that moment of success. I don't know if I ever thought you saw your greatness the way I did. I haven't changed my opinion at all. In your doing this book, I don't know if I'm any of your heroic characters or some of the interesting people you have met and shared with me. But in doing this book, if I have the chance to say a few words about you, just as an extraordinary man and taking something like dialysis and turning it into a triumph and trying to present this from the perspective and all the people you have met along the way and how you've influenced them…these are all awesome things. So, I always hope that my time with you has been helpful. I miss you in terms of seeing you. I'm always glad to have contact with you. All honor to you."

I regret so much not being able to say goodbye to Dr. Stern in person. He invited me to meet him for breakfast while I was on dialysis in 2019. I found out later he had died just a couple of weeks later.

Past, Present, Future

The summer before my senior year in college I got an unexpected call from my brother, whom I had not heard from in six years. It led to my writing a one-act play called *Reconnecting* for my senior honor's thesis about my brother coming back into my life. I held a staged reading, which received great reviews from students, professors, and administrators. I was invited to present the play at other colleges and at an arts symposium, and I even did a live broadcast on the local radio station. I believed that I had found my calling. I wanted to be a playwright and I was encouraged to write another play.

A friend of mine told me about a homeless man who carried an old violin and intermittently shouted insights to passersby at her subway stop. She passed him twice a day on her commute to and from work in Midtown Manhattan and thought the man was interesting and wondered if I could find out what his real story was. I wondered if that could be my next play.

About a week later I took the subway downtown. I was excited and a little nervous. I got off at the 53rd Street and 5th Avenue subway stop. As the train left the station, the screeching of the wheels on the tracks was replaced by the screeching of a violin in the distance. I walked slowly down the narrow empty platform.

I was following this hideous sound from the musical instrument. I steadied myself by walking alongside the red and white tiled side wall. As I glanced to read the encased platform poster, I saw the words "Masterpieces from Manet to Picasso: upstairs at MOMA." The erratic shrieking of the violin was getting louder and louder. I reached the exit sign at the end of the platform and there was a closed newsstand. Ahead were steep escalators. I was relieved for a moment not to hear the dissonance of the violin playing.

I peeked around the corner of the newsstand. Leaning against the wall and holding a violin at his side was a black man with a medium build in his thirties with smooth, milk chocolatey skin, surprisingly gleamy white teeth, and a big, bright smile. He had coarse, matted, curly, corkscrew, dark brown hair. He was wearing dirty gray sweatpants and a gray sweatshirt with the words "American Heroes" printed on it. He had a digital watch dangling from his chest and two large fanny packs strapped around his waist.

The last of the commuters scurried onto the escalator or down the steps to their connecting train. A few moments of silence were interrupted with an insight from this curious man with the violin. He shouted his words with a hint of a Caribbean accent, which echoed throughout the station, followed by a self-gratifying laugh. "O.J. was framed! A black man can't get justice in America!" I waited and did not approach. He continued, "Marriage is all about communication. Wake up! Wake up! I want to talk!"

Just then a well-dressed woman in a business suit approached him. She smiled and said, "This is for you, Carl," and handed him a glossy shopping bag. He quickly opened it and was delighted to find a fruit platter inside. Another train was pulling into the station. She said, "Have a good weekend. See you next week," as she darted toward the beeping subway doors about to close.

I listened and observed with great delight for about thirty minutes. It was an interesting interplay of sudden outbursts of twisted insights of current events and recent headlines punctuated by bursts of noise from his violin strikes. Occasionally, people walked past him and acknowledged him with a "hey" or a smile. A few people, mostly women, stopped to say something that seemed to be on their mind as if they had waited all day to tell it to him. Carl listened with his eyes and then responded in ways that seemed to provide a sense of deep understanding. Sometimes his responses were very brief but seemed to be very satisfying to these women. I could tell that they felt heard and appreciated by his undivided attention.

I decided to walk up and introduce myself. "Hi, my name is Jay. My friend told me about you. I'm interested in writing a play about the homeless."

At first, he just looked at me and studied my face. "Oh yeah. You want to write a play?" He chuckled. "I have a better story for you. O.J. was framed. Tell that story."

Was this my opening? Could this suggestion be the assignment I needed to spur me on to write again? I listened to his theory about the O.J. case.

"You're name is Carl?" I said.

He hesitated and lowered his voice to a whisper and said, "You can call me Robinson."

I headed home on the subway feeling excited on a mission to write a play about the "real" O.J. story.

I stayed up most of the night as I typed out the story on my little Macintosh computer. It was a farcical version of the events that led up to the murders and just stopped short of revealing who the real culprit was.

The next night it was pouring rain when I set out again to the depths of the subway system so that my new friend could read what I had. I found Robinson at the same spot. He stood up, leaned against the wall in the subway station, and eagerly read the nearly twenty pages that I had written. His amused snickering laughter led me to believe I was on the right track to prove his outlandish theory.

However, from the moment I first started to observe him, I had felt that Robinson was my true story. I was very taken with how smart he was and how he formed his perceptions of the world from reading the daily newspapers. First, he would twist and invert things to what he thought the real meaning of the story or topic was. Then he shared his unsolicited insights with straphangers as they moved through the station. Robinson bellowed his formulated thoughts and cackled to himself.

Sometimes people seemed entertained, other times startled or even annoyed by his rants. There was not much self-editing. It was a free flow. Free speech at its best. He had a lot to say about women. He shouted,

BAD GIRLS BAD WOMEN DON'T HAVE TIME FOR ME
PRETTY BAD BAD WOMEN RUN AWAY FROM ME
VERY BAD WOMEN ARE NO GOOD FOR ME
BAD, BAD, BAD BAD WOMEN ALL AROUND ME

After a few visits to see Robinson, I asked him to tell me a little bit about himself. He was not interested in saying too much. I pressured him a little. He told me that he had worked in an office for a couple of years and had hated it. He quit after a woman broke his heart and he decided to bypass the rest and become homeless about seven years earlier.

I started to spend more and more of my free time down in the subway station with him. Robinson was not looking for a friend, but he did not seem to mind my company. He did not panhandle. I came to realize that there was a whole community of people that in one way or another looked after him. Some stared and just experienced the daily "show" on their way to and from wherever they were going. Others bantered with him from time to time. Some people gave him food on their way to or from work. There was a nice guy who was a chef at the 21 Club nearby. He dropped off a nice piece of steak once in a while. Many others made sure that Robinson always had something to eat. I was like an extra in his live show. Mostly I watched and I waited until he took a break so that I could talk with him.

One of the other regulars who brought Robinson food was Sybil. She was an executive at a company nearby. In her forties, her hair perfectly coiffed, she wore her standard business attire with her black leather briefcase. One day she took me aside during one of Robinson's rapid-fire headline outbursts. She said, "Isn't it amazing that he keeps his sanity being homeless down here for so long?" I nodded in agreement. "How long have you known him?" I asked. Sybil told me that she had been using this subway stop for over five years. She then turned around and gave Robinson what remained of a fancy cheese and cracker tray from a business meeting that she had hosted earlier that day.

Robinson had an arrangement with Mr. Khan, the manager of the newsstand, who would let him store his violin and a bag of items overnight. In return, he swept up at closing time and helped them dispose of some empty magazine boxes from time to time. After a while, Mr. Khan and his assistant Mohammad became familiar with me.

I was curious about their perspective on things in the station. "What is the most interesting thing down here?" I asked Mr. Khan. He pointed to Robinson in the distance and in a thick Indian accent said, "He is only guy interesting here. He says all about these women and daily politics. Every time he said the same thing about women."

Well, I said, "I guess it makes your life here a little bit funnier. Mr. Khan smiled and said, "Much funny, much funny."

"How do other people react to him?" I said.

Mr. Khan looked at me very assuredly and said, "About eighty percent people enjoy him and twenty percent hate very, very much."

I said, "Hate why?"

"Because he say bad about women," Mohammed interjected. "Some woman hurt him, broke his heart. He's very intelligent, but brain damaged because of that woman who broke his heart."

I then asked, "Mohammed, do you think he would hurt anyone?"

"I don't know," he said.

"Ever see him hurt anyone?" I probed.

"Nahh…" Mr. Khan said. "Women like him especially after 6:00 pm."

Gradually, I became immersed in learning about his homeless lifestyle. Each winter, Robinson knew when the Christian missionaries were coming on certain days with a truck full of clothes, especially warm socks, and hot soup. I accompanied him up out of the subway station—or "bunker," as he sometimes referred to his home base. Swarms of needy people came from every direction toward the donation truck parked in front of the church on Fifth Avenue. I stood with Robinson as he waited his turn. One of the young volunteers had offered me socks and soup and was befuddled when I had refused them.

Each visit to see Robinson was a new and unusual experience. One day a woman in her early twenties with a bald head approached Robinson and ignored me completely. She was wearing clean blue jeans, a winter coat with a fur-lined hood, and black Converse sneakers. She hunched over slightly as her thin frame could barely support her large backpack. Lots of women approached Robinson in the station despite his negative rants about women. This one was different. She was mentally scattered and sort of star-struck in a weird kind of way. It was quite possible that she had been passing through for some time and had just built up the nerve to say something. Her speech was pressured and her thoughts were scattered. I could tell that, although my presence may have provided a sense of security at first, she no longer wanted me around. This began the recurring saga of "Baldie," as Robinson nicknamed her. She could not get enough of his attention.

The following year, I was already working on my master's degree and our conversations were mostly on the phone. I had the number to his private line right at the payphone about twenty feet from his performance space on the subway platform. I called to check in almost daily. Robinson would answer, "Headquarters. first division, second battalion, third infantry." That would crack me up. Even better, other times he would answer, "Fifth Avenue mansion. Can I help you?" It was sometimes hit or miss reaching him. Occasionally, someone walking by would pick up and say, "This is a subway station." I would quickly say, "I know, I know. Can you please just walk over and get the homeless guy standing against the wall for me?"

My conversations with Robinson often centered around his many brilliant inventions and ideas. He was obsessed with my helping him get a patent on his model of time travel. Robinson would say, "Just send it in to the patent office. You will be on Ted Koppel in no time."

I asked him to explain it to me. He said, "Look, the timewave surrounds everything like water. It's like having the entire city under water. The time wave surrounds things and that is why you can't travel through time. The reason why the past, present, and future happen at the same time is so that we can't change anything. Time is a human concept. The first day and the last day are the same. As far as the universe is concerned this is still the first day. The universe doesn't have a time sequence. In time travel there is no past. There is no present. There is no future. Time travel is based on the constant acceleration of light."

On one of my many visits to the subway station I wanted to see if he was really serious about all of this. I told Robinson that he would have to have a working model of something before I could submit anything to the patent office. He gave me a paper with a diagram on it. It said "Past, Present, Future" with a big X at a certain angle on the page. He was insistent. "Just send it in. Only I know these principles for time travel. Those boys will know what I am talking about. There is a post office two blocks away. Just do it. It's a couple dollars certified mail."

I pointed to a five-dollar bill that someone had dropped into his violin case. He smirked and said, "There are certain things that I just can't do, and besides you're my assistant anyway." I laughed. A train was pulling into the station, and as I stepped onto the subway car, Robinson's next thought bellowed out of him.

AFTER FIFTY YEARS THE WOMAN OF MY DREAMS
STILL LOOKS YOUNG AND BEAUTIFUL...
THE WOMAN OF MY DREAMS STAYS IN MY DREAMS...
WHERE IT DOESN'T COST A PENNY TO DREAM!

One memorable time Robinson came to the phone and I could hear some commotion and a woman screaming at him half in English and half in Spanish. Then Robinson dropped the phone and I heard a man's voice say, "Put your hands behind your back." There was a Spanish woman who would sometimes steal his spot on the platform when Robinson would wander off and she would start playing her guitar there. This had become a bone of contention. Apparently, the violin and guitar players were not a good match. The woman called the police to say she had been assaulted. He ended up spending two nights at Riker's Island until it was all sorted out. I wrote a letter on his behalf that I had been on the phone with him the whole time when this alleged incident took place, and he was released.

One thing remained constant day after day. Robinson was the attraction. His position in life made it interesting. He was pure, not motivated by monetary gain, fame, or fortune, and secluded 120 feet below street level society in his bunker. Yet his knowledge and perspective from afar filtered through. Robinson saw the world through a tinted window. He glared out at people on their daily shuttle through life. Some passersby were pulled off course a little and made to reflect on their lives. It was this distraction created by Robinson that made this possible. However, I was always thinking of ways to get him to join society with me since I enjoyed spending time with him.

One night I really wanted to see the Mondrian exhibit upstairs at MOMA. It was hard to get in. There was a constant line down the block and you needed tickets. I kept begging Robinson to come out of the "bunker" and to the museum with me. Finally, he relented. We went upstairs and to the street and literally just walked down the block. There was a massive crush of people lined up at the box office and a ticketholder's line with a two-hour wait to get in. It was sold out. I was looking for Robinson when I heard a "Yo, Jay" coming from the entrance area and turned around. One of Robinson's friends who worked security there had recognized him from his daily subway commute and got him in free of charge. I was being waved in as his guest! It seemed he had pull everywhere we went. As I breezed past everyone in their leather coats and cashmere scarfs on the line, I got some quizzical looks. I had connections.

One of the biggest snowstorms hit in the winter of 1996 in New York City, where I was now teaching at a public school. Schools closed for a couple of days in the city, which was unheard of. I made my way to the subway to see Robinson. He saw that I was wearing sneakers and said, "Where are your boots? What are you, stupid? Do you want to fall and crack your head open?" The next day we took an adventure to Paragon Sporting Goods near 14th Street. I bought him a new pair of Kodiak boots and a pair for myself. We matched.

Sometimes our adventures had undetermined destinations. I just followed to see where we would end up. In the beginning, maybe he was just trying to see if he could lose me along the way. We took many trips down to Chinatown. There was a particular rice milk at a produce market that Robinson liked a lot. There was a movie theater with martial arts and action shows with subtitles that seemed to really tickle his fancy. Robinson would mimic the unsynchronized mouth movements and sounds from these poorly made productions. That is how I discovered that he loved going to the movies. In the mainstream theaters, he loved action and adventure movies, especially ones with conspiratorial and scientific plots. He would not go for romantic comedies or anything like that.

We started going to the movies together from time to time. Sometimes the subway rides were awkward in that Robinson would continue his show on the train, shouting his twisted thoughts and jokes, which were often inappropriate both in language and taste. I would be standing right next to him and suddenly he would start to blurt out things that made me feel very uncomfortable. It was part of the deal of hanging out with him. The routine was to go to 34th Street Penn Station and walk to the multiplex theater.

First, we would stop at a Chinese takeout place and get food. Robinson would have no problem walking in with his bag of food and I followed along. He would go to the very front of the theater and start eating. He made himself right at home and I followed his every move. At the end of the movie as the credits were rolling, I would look over to say something to him and he would be gone. Robinson was like a ninja. Poof. That would usually be the end of our day together. He would sometimes sneak into the next theater without a trace or maybe he just needed space. Other times, our adventures continued.

I explored areas of the city I had never seen before. He was not always comfortable going into certain restaurants so I would have to go in and get the food to go. He had good taste and was a connoisseur of specialty foods and drinks. I don't think anyone had hung out with him like I did. There was no real warm and fuzzy, but I wanted to experience everything I could until I was too tired or the conversation dried up.

Frequently, people who traveled through the station were lost and needed directions. Robinson knew his way around the subway system like the back of his hand. While he was eager to help when he saw someone in distress, people could be a little bit leery of him at times. When I was standing there with him one day a strikingly attractive, tall black woman approached me to ask which train to take and ignored Robinson. She was fashionably dressed and looked like a model. I thought I was helping by directing her to take the E train and she thanked me as it pulled in. Robinson was nudging me toward the edge of the platform alongside the woman. She got on the train and at the last moment, as the doors were closing, he pushed me onto the train with her.

I spoke to her for a few minutes as the train swayed and lurched from side to side. I asked her for her number and surprisingly she gave it to me. A few days later, I called her and asked her to meet me for dinner the following Saturday at the Europa Café on 57th Street, which was diagonally across from Carnegie Hall. I wore my button-down Polo dress shirt and khakis. I was not sure if she would show up after waiting for about twenty-five minutes. I was losing hope and then suddenly the gorgeous woman appeared in the doorway wearing a tight black dress.

We had a huge slice of chocolate cake for dessert and she fed it to me. After dinner we walked down Central Park South past luxury buildings, and the doormen's heads were turning to get a glimpse first of this beautiful woman on my arm and then to see what lucky guy was with her. We sat on the edge of a fountain near Rockefeller Center and started to make out. I had a confidence about me that night.

We entered Robinson's subway station for the trip home. I was hoping he would still be up to see me walk by with her. We took the long escalator ride down to the bunker where he was sprawled out and sleeping in front of the newsstand. As we walked the short distance to the stairs leading down to the uptown train, I peeked over and at the very last moment he opened one eye and saw us go by. I think he approved.

As my confidence grew, I decided to take a standup comedy class and started to perform at various comedy clubs around the city. My friend who worked on *The David Letterman Show* helped me get booked at Caroline's Comedy Club later that year. I invited Robinson to come see me perform. It was a long shot. He did not go out to upscale places like that. He was picky about where he went and what he did. However, he did break the "fourth wall" and came out of the bunker unexpectedly. I had told him that I would leave him a ticket at the door with some cash for food and drinks. I told the hostess to be on the lookout just in case he showed up.

The lights were very bright when I was up on stage. I only saw a few people in the front while performing. I heard Robinson's cackle and looked over during my set and there he was. The infamous comedian of the subway had come out to see me perform. We flipped the script. It was a thrill for me to share this moment with Robinson just a few blocks from where we hung out at the spot.

In the late '90s after getting married and moving to New Jersey I saw less of Robinson. I was still teaching in New York City but commuting. I went from trying my hand at performing standup comedy to producing professional standup shows in the city. I rented out a small theater at the Producer's Club on 44th Street and enjoyed going around to different comedy clubs to scout out talent and promoting my shows.

When my daughter Lizzie was born, I really wanted to share the news with Robinson. My wife and I drove into the city with the baby and I parked outside the station. I went down to the bunker and found Robinson. He returned up to street level with me to meet my wife and new daughter. It might have been a little awkward for him, but he was happy for me. I took a leave of absence from my teaching job and started a speakers bureau, providing motivational and inspirational assembly programs for schools. Once that got off the ground, I was very busy and lost touch for a while with Robinson.

Amazingly, a couple of years later, I read an article about him in the *New York Times*. It was truly an amazing tribute to Robinson, who had his throat slashed when he was sleeping one night at his usual spot. He had stumbled to that same payphone where we had talked so many times and called 911 as he was bleeding to death. Paramedics reached him just in time to get him to a nearby hospital.

His absence at the subway station caused quite a stir. He was missed by many during that very next day's rush hour after the attack. According to the article, it was Sybil who had called all of the local hospitals until she found Robinson and went to visit him. Mohammed at the newsstand posted a sign, much to the relief of his subway supporters, that Robinson was alive and well. I was determined to find more time to spend with Robinson after reading the article.

I attended a conference in New York City at the Sheraton hotel just a few blocks away from Robinson's spot. During the break time Robinson was on my mind. I had not spoken with him in a while so I walked down 53rd Street and went down into the subway and asked the woman attendant in the token booth if she had seen Carl the homeless man. He was not your usual homeless guy. People knew him. At first, she did not seem to know who I was talking about. I think she suspected that he might be in some sort of trouble and did not want to give out any information. I was wearing a suit and who knows what she thought. I explained how many years that I had known him. She then told me that she had seen him the day before.

The attendant also went on to tell me that she had been confidentially communicating with Robinson's mother, who from time to time had come down looking for him since reading the article in the newspaper. The attendant was giving updates to the mother. I was shocked to learn that his mother was still interested in looking for him after all those years and wondered if Robinson even knew that his mother had been around. I left my business card with the attendant at the token booth and she promised to be in touch when she made contact with him again.

A couple of weeks later, the attendant called me and said to be expecting a call soon. Robinson called me on my 800 number and we arranged to meet up.

Robinson related that after 9/11 most of the people who had looked after him and had sustained him on a daily basis with food and provisions left the city for good. For the almost decade and a half that he had been living down in the subway, he had never panhandled. He was in permanent residence as performer, therapist, comedian, futurist, philosopher, and odd institution in the subway station. After the terrorist attacks, Robinson was forced to leave his bunker each evening, and he began a new run just a few blocks away on 57th Street outside the high-end Japanese Nobu restaurant. His legend grew as he rubbed elbows with famous athletes, actors, royalty, and other very wealthy patrons as they came and went from that restaurant's exclusive dining rooms.

I spent many nights outside Nobu talking with Robinson in those later years. I would drive in from New Jersey after dinner and park in front of the place next to the limousines and Escalades. Cameron Diaz was a big fan of Robinson. At the time, she was dating

Alex Rodriguez. A-Rod was annoyed that he would have to stand off to the side as Cameron spoke to him. They had seven "meetings." Robinson would buy sparkly rings at a wholesale place downtown so that he could give out gifts to generous patrons, who handed him tens, twenties, and even hundred-dollar bills at times. He placed a ring on Cameron's finger one night and she proudly wore it home.

I was able to spot many celebrities while Robinson gave stock tips to wealthy guys who actually listened to his insights. "Hey, Robinson, there's Chris Rock!" I said, as Chris darted out of the restaurant to his black Porsche parked out front. Robinson turned and rushed back toward the car, hoping for a bill or two. Lionel Richie spent ten minutes with us after dinner one night just talking casually. It was not a big deal to be with Robinson and have Alec Baldwin or a Saudi Royal family member stop by to talk.

I was still a somewhat good assistant. Robinson was an expert on the best sanitary wipes available on the market. This item was crucial to his homeless lifestyle. He needed to stay fresh. It turned out that ShopRite brand cleansing wipes were the most effective for cleanliness without irritating his skin. I bought them by the case and brought them with me on a regular basis. One night I was handing him the individual packages, which he would store in the inner pockets of his overcoat. The well-dressed restaurant security guard's eyes darted from the entrance to our exchange of packages, probably suspecting a drug deal going down.

I returned many times to see Robinson and I recorded some of our conversations at the end of his busy nights hobnobbing with the rich and famous. We would walk back to the bunker together and I would pepper Robinson with questions that he rarely wanted to answer but thought would be good to have in my memory bank. Robinson was not always a warm and fuzzy kind of guy. He could be brutal with his comments or feedback. Begrudgingly, though, he answered my questions.

I asked him, "What was your experience with Jay over the years?" Robinson did not hesitate as he sat on the ground at his performance spot with his head tilted back on the tiled subway station wall, where I had spent so many days with him over the years. I braced myself.

"Well, the experience with Jay is like *Saving Private Ryan*. Saving Jay. That's what it was all about. Saving Jay. Jay came out here to save the world and didn't know he needed to be saved. So, his adventure in saving the world ended up saving Jay and that's how it worked out."

"What about my standup comedy?" I asked.

Robinson said, "I saw him do that. He had the natural body for it but he never pursued it. Again, one of his never pursued great dreams."

"What does the future hold for Jay?"

With a devilish grin on his face he said, "The future holds for Jay?... To be arrested by Homeland Security for being a threat to national security. Jay, seriously, people love you. They love you and like you. They think you're a great guy and they give up the secrets when they meet you."

I could tell Robinson had enough of my questions and he pivoted back to his favorite topic of time travel. "One of the mistakes that movies about time travel make is that if you travel through time and you leave the time machine behind, how are you going get back? It is like going into the desert and leaving your car behind. How are you going to get back? You ever notice that this is a classic mistake in time travel movies? People travel through time but the machine is left back in the lab. Remember you needed a machine to time travel so if you need a machine to time travel why did you leave the machine back in the lab? That's a laughable point about time travel. It makes it real funny. You have to take the machine with you. It's like a spaceship. Wherever you go you take it with you. A time travel machine must be taken with you or else you can't come back to the point of origin."

I was tired and said goodbye, and as I took the steep escalator back up to the world above, my eyes fixated on an empty framed space on the wall with no poster, just the words: "New Exhibit in Creation."

* * *

I had not been able to connect with Robinson prior to my move from New Jersey to Pennsylvania in 2015. While in New York City for an appointment in 2018, I went down into the subway station and spoke to the current manager of the newsstand to inquire about "Carl." The man looked at me and acted as if he had no idea who I was talking about. I was a little worried at first that maybe something had happened to Robinson. The manager's attitude changed after I took out my phone and showed multiple photos to prove my friendship was real. He then said, "I saw him last night." I was so relieved and left my business card and a note with the manager and he promised to give it to Robinson the next time he encountered him.

Two months later I received a call on my 800 number from a New York number that I did not recognize. I checked the voicemail and much to my surprise was a message from Robinson. He said, "Hey, Jay man. How you been? What's going good with you? Yeah, I got your card. I heard you've been looking for me. I'll try to get in touch with you again."

I quickly dialed back the number on the caller ID and he answered! We spoke for at least two hours on the phone catching up. I had never had such a long conversation with him on the phone. I related to him that my kidneys had failed and that I was now on dialysis. I told him that I would drive into the city that next Monday and meet him on 34th Street at the movie theater we usually went to years before.

On the morning of our meeting I received another message from him. "It's Monday. Don't forget." I set out and I was almost to New York City that day and received a third call from Robinson, which I picked up as I was about thirty minutes outside of New York City. "You're still coming, right?" After treating him to dinner, we saw the *Black Panther* movie that evening and Robinson was ready to surf to another theater for the next movie.

My personal connection with Robinson made me feel like I was that one in a billion person who had hit the lottery. I got to peek behind that hidden door of genius that led to his extraordinarily creative mind. It was an up-close and personal relationship with a living treasure of a person. Robinson was in the small group of lifelong connections who could see the potential inside me. Even through his brutal honesty, I always knew he still cared and hoped for the best for me.

Shadow Boxing

I sat next to a skinny African American guy in his mid- to late thirties named Kenny when I first started dialysis. He usually wore saggy, faded acid-wash jeans, a white T-shirt, and clean white sneakers. Kenny usually strolled in at least fifteen minutes late for his scheduled treatments. There was always some commotion in the room as to if and when Kenny would show up as the staff tried their best to keep to their shift schedule.

For the first few weeks, Kenny and I merely exchanged friendly nods as the staff ushered him to his chair. He usually only stayed awake for a few minutes after being connected to the dialysis machine. After that Kenny just snored heavily for four hours until the end of his treatment. I was not a sleeper. It was noontime and I could not stand the loud snoring that was coming from just a few feet away. He seemingly stopped breathing for long periods of time and often exploded periodically with gasping sounds.

The only thing I could think of this one day was to try to engage Kenny in a conversation that could potentially distract him from sleeping. I wanted to delay the loud honking for as long as possible. I thought I would try this before I asked to be switched to another chair location. So, this one day, I asked him to tell me a little bit about himself.

Kenny said, "My dad was a semipro boxer. I grew up in a boxing gym my whole life."

"How come your dad didn't go pro?" I said.

"After a few fights he got injured," Kenny said. "Then he trained and sparred with pro boxers for years. He trained me to fight too."

I said, "So, you became a boxer like your dad?"

"Nah, but I used it to fight to survive inside."

"What do you mean?" I said.

Kenny looked at me with a sort of perpetually exhausted look on his face. He said, "I had to fight for my life every day for the first year in prison."

This led to a long series of very graphic episodes in which Kenny described how he had to use his boxing skills that he had learned from his dad to survive each day.

"It was a knockout every day," he said. "Until bigger and stronger inmates began challenging me and I started getting knocked out. Eventually, I joined a gang to survive and also fixed people's TVs and radios on the side, so people didn't really mess with me too much after a while."

As he told the prison stories, I was relieved to not hear his snoring, but his blood pressure reading skyrocketed and he was sweating profusely. The nurse rushed over. It was clear that he needed to stop the prison stories. What had I triggered? The beeping of his machine was getting louder and louder, which alerted the staff to the crisis situation.

A nurse darted over with IV fluid bags used to deliver relief for his cramps. Everyone begged him to change the subject. Once his blood pressure stabilized, Kenny turned to me and said, "I was just released from prison a few months ago."

I was not eager to ask him what he had been in for. "How did you get dialysis while you were in prison?"

"I refused treatment," he said. "But then it got really bad so with eight years left on my sentence I was released so that I could get medical care. I also had my sentence reduced for being part of the prison outreach group that speaks to kids about not doing drugs."

Kenny and I sort of became friends after that. I had an extra ticket and invited him to go with me to a fundraiser at a local college where some sports legends assembled to raise money for a local scholarship foundation. Kenny lived with his mom in a bad section of town. He did not have a car so I picked him up. It seemed like Kenny had a good time at the event. We met some ballplayers and listened to acceptance speeches from the inner-city students who received scholarships that night.

On the ride home Kenny told me that he did not qualify to get on the list for a kidney transplant due to some sort of illness in his lungs. He told me, "I been researching about this new artificial kidney they came up with out in California."

I said, "I read an article about that too. They have been working on that at the University of San Francisco and I think they need just a few million dollars to complete the trials."

"I've been tryin' to get registered to be in the trial," he said. "But no one ever called me back. That might be my only chance...getting an artificial kidney."

I noticed that the social worker and other staff at the dialysis center sometimes dropped off plastic bags or envelopes next to his machine from time to time when Kenny was sleeping. He usually put the stuff in his duffle bag quietly before he went home and never said too much. Apparently, Kenny had been kicked out of the house by his mother.

The snoring was just too much for me so I took another chair on the other side of the room. Kenny found an apartment not long after that but had no furniture. My wife and I brought him a desk, lamp, chair, and other essential items. He managed to buy a used electric scooter, which he used as transportation to travel the five miles to dialysis. It was like a skateboard with a little motor connected to a thin handlebar. Kenny had to balance carefully to not only navigate traffic but people who threw bottles and garbage out their car windows at him.

I had asked Kenny early on to bring in some photos from his dad's boxing days, which he did. We sat in the lobby one day and looked through some tattered black and white photos and Polaroids. I was surprised that he had remembered. He said, "I asked my mom if I could look through some old boxes at her house." Kenny took a lot of time to describe exactly who was in each photo and what was going on. Most of the photos were taken at the boxing gym. In one photo a young Kenny stood behind his dad, who held the heavy training bag as a heavyweight boxer launched a knockout blow at the bag in a training session. Kenny still had the same worried expression on his face that he had in that childhood photo.

A few weeks later, Kenny disappeared. It was a mystery as to what had happened to him. About a month later, during my treatment, I overheard a nurse relate to another staff member, "Kenny turned up in California. The hospital is requesting his records." I thought to myself, *How did he end up in California?*

Months later, with not much fanfare, Kenny returned to the dialysis center. He acted like he had never been gone. Kenny was barely able to walk, even with a cane, and was even skinnier than before. It was shocking to see how much he had deteriorated. Kenny did not speak to me or anyone for weeks. I gave him space as I could tell he had been through something traumatic. After one of his treatments, he approached my chair when no one was around and told me the whole story.

Kenny said, "I bought a bus ticket to California with the last money I had. I wanted to get out there and go to the research center in San Francisco to get my name on the list for the artificial kidney." He looked down at the floor and said, "It was my last chance."

"How did you get dialysis on the way?" I asked.

"I didn't. I just got on the bus and tried to make it there," he said. "It took longer than I thought with all the layovers and I ran out of cash."

I nervously asked, "What happened?"

Kenny said, "Someone found me unconscious in the back of the bus and I ended up in the ICU in Los Angeles for three weeks. When I was discharged, I stayed in a homeless shelter until I got the energy to hitchhike to San Francisco. I never made it to the research center. I got a job washing dishes at a restaurant in L.A., slept at the shelter, and got dialysis in the clinic at the hospital." He said, "I had gotten another scooter to get around town there. A car ran into me and I went flying up in the air and landed headfirst and broke both of my arms." Kenny lifted his arms up to show me the scars.

"That's terrible, Kenny. How did you get back to the East Coast?" I asked.

"My mom sent me the money for a bus ticket home," he said.

I looked at Kenny's frail body as he leaned on his cane in front of my dialysis chair. He was but a shadow of his former self. Kenny had a hard-luck life. I simultaneously felt sorry for him and looked up to him for his extraordinary efforts considering the lack of resources that were available to him. He was determined to find a way to live against all odds. All of us in that room were in the same boat. A friend once told me, "All of us earthlings are on this boat together, and life is hard for most people, but everyone should be accepted and understood."

Ordinary Becomes Extraordinary

By the time my daughter Lizzie was a junior in high school, she and I were both on "tour" together while I was still on dialysis. I made it to all but one of her college campus tours, and she was my companion for most of my Reconnection Tour. Sometimes our tours overlapped in unique ways. We spent one of her college visit days at Drew University in New Jersey. There was an evening reception in their art gallery. I recognized a face in the crowd. I said to myself, *Wait a second. Is that Dave Terdiman?* I looked down at his name tag and said, "Dave, it's me, Jay Gittleson." It was really an unexpected reconnection.

Dave, just a few years older than me, had been the director of the Hillel, which was the student organization for Jewish life on my own college campus in the mid-1990s. There was a small chapel that we shared with the Christian ministry. As student president of the Hillel, I helped Dave promote our events on campus, and soon that little chapel started to fill up for Friday night Shabbat dinners and Jewish holiday celebrations. Even some curious non-Jewish friends attended. Among other group activities, we took a trip to Ellis Island and helped fundraise for Jewish causes.

After I graduated, I continued at FDU for my master's degree and stayed involved with the Hillel. Dave told me about a ten-day mission trip to Israel hosted by the United Jewish Appeal, which included graduate students from around the country. All Dave asked was that I share some of my experiences from the trip upon my return with certain temples or Jewish groups that had supported the mission trip.

Many of the graduate students on the trip were from top universities like Stanford and Harvard. I felt a little bit insecure as cliques formed on the trip. I tried to talk to a cute blond girl who was on my tour bus wearing a *Yale Law* sweatshirt. I asked, "How do you like Yale?" She glanced at my *FDU* sweatshirt and just snarled at me, "Can't you see you're interrupting our conversation?" She rolled her eyes and then ignored me. The girl sitting next to her laughed and I felt so hurt. It was more than just what school I went to but that I had missed the natural progression of milestones in my life as a young man or they had been severely delayed. I never had a girlfriend. It felt so far off to me and I was also self-conscious about my being overweight throughout my life. Even as things became more stable and I encountered women who may have been interested in me, my lack of experience made it hard for me to pick up on female cues. I felt emotionally wounded by that girl on the bus and may have missed out on talking to other nicer ones on the trip.

There were some unexpected and miraculous things that happened while I was in Israel. After we spent the first night on a kibbutz near the Sea of Galilee, our tour bus driver took us to a historical site called The Valley of Tears. That was the name given to an area in the Golan Heights after it became the site of a major battle in the 1973 Yom Kippur War. A little bleary-eyed from the long trip, I stood next to a commemorative plaque that overlooked the battle site. Just then, an Israeli guy who was a student from my university approached me. I wondered why he was on this trip with American students visiting Israel for the first time. He ran up to me and said, "Your friend Jerry is very sick. He has leukemia. He might not be alive by the time we get back." I was in shock and on the verge of tears in the Valley of Tears.

Jerry was my only friend from high school, and we had not been in regular contact for a while. He was pretty much a loner living with his mother. I last saw Jerry about eight months earlier in a lecture hall at the university where I had a dramatic reading of my one-act play, which was my senior honor's thesis. Right before the start of the performance, Jerry suddenly entered the room and rushed over to me. He said, "I fell off my bicycle on the way over." I remembered that I was nervous and sort of brushed him off and whispered, "I'll talk to you afterwards."

It was the first full day of a ten-day trip. I called Jerry from Israel. He said, "I have leukemia and I am sick with PCP pneumonia. I'm in an experimental cancer treatment program in New York City."

I asked, "When did you get diagnosed?"

Jerry said, "Well, I had swollen lymph nodes and decided to go to the emergency room. They did an emergency bone marrow test and found out that I had leukemia.

"Why didn't you tell me?" I asked.

Jerry said, "Well, I don't know. It's been crazy."

I said, "Love you and I'll see you when I get back."

I had to go all the way to Israel, to find out what was happening with my friend who lived in the same town in New Jersey. *Would I make it back in time?*

We visited other sites and sometimes had a guest speaker who came on the bus and shared their insights. We heard from a man named Zohar, an Ethiopian Jew who had fled with other persecuted refugees to Israel in the 1980s. He had been sponsored by an American family whose financial support enabled him to receive housing, schooling, books, and supplies as he got settled. Zohar explained that he had received many letters from this caring family and felt they were truly his saviors. I found his inspirational story fascinating.

When all the students got off the bus, I went up to Zohar. I said to him, "Where was that family from that supported you?"

Zohar said, "The family was from New Orleans, Louisiana."

"That's interesting because my family is from New Orleans," I said. "My mother was born and raised there. I lived there for a few years too. What was the name of the family?"

When he said the last name, I was overcome. It was my family! My great uncle had funded and supported Zohar all those years. We were both in a little bit of shock for a moment as we realized we had this special connection.

During the trip, our tour bus driver was a stoic older man in his late fifties. I spoke to him frequently during our layovers and asked him about his life. I learned that he was a retired Israeli Army officer and a highly decorated war hero. To me, he silently became more than a bus driver but our protector. I found it very striking that he was sort of overlooked and ignored by the students on the trip. I looked forward to my daily conversations with him.

On the last day of the trip, as we toured a rehabilitation center for people with disabilities, I was approached by one of the group coordinators. She asked, "Would you reflect on your experiences from the trip and share some of your thoughts with the entire group after lunch?" I was a little nervous but agreed to speak to the group of about two hundred people. I had about thirty minutes to collect my thoughts. It came to me very quickly.

I shared with the group about my dying friend, my family connection to the Ethiopian refugee, and I explained that we had a war hero as a bus driver. I looked out at the group, which had become quiet and focused on me. I said, "What seems so ordinary could be so extraordinary."

The girl who had been rude to me earlier in the trip darted over to me right after I finished speaking. She said, "That was amazing. I'm sorry that I didn't talk to you earlier and get to know you better on the trip."

It's Personal

When I was in graduate school, I saw a flyer for an assertiveness training class held at the university counseling center on campus. It was more of a support group of sorts where people shared how their weekly interactions with others were going. Group members offered advice to each other, and the resident psychologist guided the discussion.

There was one guy in the group named Peter who was on the shy side and was very soft-spoken during the sessions. He was a doctoral candidate in clinical psychology. One day I saw Peter walking on campus wearing a black leather biker jacket with a motorcycle helmet in his hand. I said hello but he seemed oblivious to the world around him as his leather boots pounded the pavement. He was a clean-cut, fit guy about six feet tall with perfectly combed short brown hair, blue eyes, and a clean-shaven face. Inside the support group he seemed so approachable, but on those occasions where I saw him outside of the group, he gave off a completely different vibe.

I approached Peter one day and asked him why he had ignored me when I passed him on the walkway. He seemed shocked and assured me that he had not seen me. He also seemed to want to be friends after that. We hung out a few times. I went on to finish my master's degree and took a job teaching at a school in New York City while he completed his doctoral dissertation.

One day I got a call from Peter. He told me that he wanted to meet a woman and had decided that his best shot was to place a personal ad in the local newspaper. Since he knew that I was an English teacher and a good writer, Peter thought to ask me if I could help him craft something that would land him the woman of his dreams. He liked what I had written for him so much that he insisted that I write an ad for myself so that I could also meet someone special.

I said, "Peter, I live in New York City. Why would I place an ad in a New Jersey paper?" He said, "Jay, I really think that you should. You have a way with words. Give it a try." I decided to take his advice. Little did I know that my life would be forever changed.

My ad read:

SENSITIVE GUY
Caring, romantic SWM, beautiful blue eyes, N/S, teacher, sensitive, into the arts, love kids, seeks a mature woman, to share special times with.

I received several responses from the ad from older single moms with kids. In my third year of teaching at twenty-seven years old, perhaps the wording of my ad could have been a bit better. Then I received a message in my personals voicemail from a woman named Ellen who seemed very nice. She was a speech pathologist working in a hospital setting in New Jersey and in her late thirties with no children. Since she lived in a suburb about twenty minutes outside of New York City, I asked her if she would come into the city to meet me for dinner. She said, "Jay, why don't you come to Rutherford to meet me. There is a train station and bus stop right in the center of town."

I agreed, and the following Friday evening I took the bus in to meet her. I was wearing a Polo shirt, khakis, and my brown preppie leather buck shoes. As I exited the bus, I recognized Ellen as she said she would be wearing a leopard print skirt. We hugged and she said, "Do you want to go to Hoboken for appetizers?" She tossed me the keys to her brand-new Toyota Camry as she said, "Here, you drive." I was surprised and excited.

She had grown up in Hoboken, New Jersey, which at that point had become a yuppie destination with clubs and restaurants just across from the New York City skyline. We parked along the main drag on Washington Street and walked to a nearby Chinese restaurant for an egg roll, then crossed the street to hear singing servers over hamburgers at Johnny Rockets.

I found out from Ellen that Hoboken's one square mile held a lot of history. She showed me the plaque at the location where the first baseball game was played on June 19, 1846. We drove along the waterfront area called Frank Sinatra Drive. As we passed the street sign, Ellen told me, "My mother sat right behind her good friend Frank Sinatra in class at Demarest High School. Our family also had a summer home in Rumson and socialized with the Sinatras from time to time."

Our conversation was easy and relaxed. "I was a miracle baby," she said. "One of my family nicknames growing up was 'The Tumor.'" Apparently, her mother Elizabeth, already in her forties with four children, had felt something unusual in her abdomen. Her doctors determined that there was a floating fibroid tumor that needed to be surgically removed as soon as possible. On the operating table, a doctor thought to take an X-ray, which revealed that the rapidly growing tumor was actually a baby soon to be named Ellen!

I told Ellen, "The buses stop running at 12 midnight. There is no way I can get back to New York City."

She did not hesitate. "You can stay over at my home, which I share with my mother."

I slept on the basement pull-out sofa, of course, and met her mom Elizabeth, or "Mertie," in the morning on her way out to her weekly appointment to the beauty parlor. Little did I know that there had been a frantic warning that night from her mom that I could have been an ax murderer. Ellen was instructed to lock the bedroom doors and the basement door. In the morning there were fresh warm bagels, scrambled eggs, and juice waiting for me upstairs. I walked up through the basement door, which had no lock installed on it.

I thought that our second date should be in New York City. It was the middle of the summer so I think that Ellen was a little confused when I told her, "Bring along a warm sweater." I met her at the Port Authority bus station and hailed a cab going uptown. When we arrived at the Ed Sullivan Theater, Ellen looked up at the marquis and said, "You have tickets to see the Letterman Show?" We bypassed the ticketholders' line and went right to the front door and in for rehearsals as my friend Bill, David Letterman's head of security at the theater, escorted us right into the chilly, overly air-conditioned theater under those hot studio lights.

Ellen did eventually make it to my apartment in upper Manhattan. She decided to hang out there one day while I was at a conference. When I returned and opened the door, I thought that I had entered the wrong apartment. She had completely cleaned the place from top to bottom and organized everything. It was a new life for me. To repay her, I dragged Ellen around to various comedy clubs as I was trying to practice material for a performance at a new talent night at Caroline's Comedy Club that upcoming fall. She was not much of a standup comedy fan, but she knew it meant a lot to me.

One day I got a call from Ellen. She said, "I slipped and fell outside while decorating for the holidays and broke my leg. It took some time for the ambulance to get here as my mother called her eighty-year-old sister instead of 911. Her sister then called for help but gave the wrong address."

Once at the hospital, "Mertie" tried unsuccessfully to call me from the cordless phone that she had carried with her from the house. She did assist the ER doctor at the understaffed hospital as she held Ellen's leg as it was set for the cast.

Ellen and I became much closer after that as I picked her up from work each day in her car, which she loaned me. A few months later, Ellen invited me to move in and I gave up my apartment in the city and decided to commute to work just over the George Washington Bridge.

Two years exactly from the date that we met, Ellen and I were married on July 11, 1999 in our living room, presided over by the mayor of our town. I asked my old friend, Mike the Clown, to be my best man. Our reception was under a tent in the backyard, and the back deck was our dance floor with a one-man band.

Ellen wore a corsage on her right wrist to cover the scar from a cat bite that she had received a few weeks before the wedding, which landed her in the hospital for a week. Apparently, I had forgotten to close the screen door to the backyard and Ellen's honey bear cat named Troy left the house for the first time ever. Troy had simply walked around the house and was waiting at the front door because he realized it was much better indoors. Ellen came home and saw her silver cat outside, freaked out, and grabbed its tail. The surprised feline bit into Ellen's hand so deeply that the ensuing infection required emergency surgery to save her hand.

Not to be outdone, the next day my mother-in-law sliced her hand open cleaning the china closet and required emergency surgery to save her hand. I spent a whole night in the hospital waiting room taking calls from Ellen's family while they got ready for a big shindig in south Jersey and were too busy to be there.

On January 1, 2001 our amazing gift from God was born as our beautiful daughter Elizabeth, "Lizzie," entered the world.

* * *

Peter was at our home in Rutherford and met Lizzie as an infant in 2001. We lost touch. I did not see him again until 2018 when I reached out to him while on dialysis. He had been married and had a fourteen-year-old son who lived with him. Peter drove up to our home in Pennsylvania to visit. He accompanied me to my friend's nearby home who had a yearly get-together. When we walked in, former heavyweight boxing champion Larry Holmes was standing in the living room. Larry, who lived locally, posed for a photo with Peter and later spontaneously shared his life story out on the back deck. Peter slept over in our guest room and we went out for lunch the next day. It was quite a memorable reconnection along my tour.

Dream Fulfilled

There was a lot of anxiety when a dialysis technician approached me with those very long needles to insert into the access or fistula in my right arm, which was my lifeline. It was the way in which the blood flowed out of my body and into my artificial kidney or filter that was attached to the dialysis machine. My blood was then cleaned and returned to my body.

It was the luck of the draw which technician was on duty and assigned to my area or "pod" on any given day. I believed after a while that no matter what training a tech had, it was a talent that someone either possessed or struggled to master.

I did have my favorite techs at my center. Tara was not one of them. She was an attractive woman about five feet six in her late thirties, with sparkling green eyes and a long mane of voluminous brown hair down to her back. She was curvy and walked with a wiggle around the center. Her loud and sometimes obnoxious personality and her lack of self-awareness in some ways entertained me. She was like in her own bubble.

In the beginning, she did not seem to see me or even notice that I was there. I tried to be friendly. If she walked by my dialysis chair, I said hello. When she did respond, it was as if she could not figure me out and so just paid as little attention to me as possible. Tara flitted around the room and seemed more concerned with gossip than with anything else. Her one attempt at sticking my arm with the needles had not gone well so I think we had mutually agreed to stay away from each other.

Over time, though, Tara and I spoke on occasion and I could see that she cared deeply in her own special way for the patients. I had come to understand that she was a mother of two teenaged boys and a three-year-old daughter. She told me that she used to be an aide in a nursing home and was very proud to have become a dialysis technician. Her strong point was that she took the time to talk with patients about things that were happening in her life, which helped make emotional connections and lightened the mood in the room.

Tara also loved to cook and bake. One patient heard about her special potato salad and put in a special request for his birthday. Sure enough, she delivered a bowl of it to him as promised. She also loved to sing and she frequently turned up the boom box in the room and sang along, which was always a highlight for the patients. In fact, Tara, now in her late thirties, explained that she had previously auditioned for *The Voice* and twice for *American Idol*.

One afternoon I was getting a treatment as Tara took care of a patient two chairs away from me. It was hard to have a private conversation in an open room like that, so my attention was drawn to Tara as she basically told the story of her early life to those within earshot on that side of the room. I was riveted to what she said. Her voice was steady and she was unashamed to share her extremely personal story.

Tara said, "My mother was a drug addict. She abandoned me when I was a young child and I was put into foster care. I hated it. When I was twelve years old, I stole my foster parent's car and drove away. I was later arrested and put into juvenile detention and in the system for many years."

It was heartbreaking. I looked over in Tara's direction and our eyes locked. It was as if there was an imaginary tube being connected from my heart to hers like the ones sending my blood through the dialysis machine. In that moment, I wanted so much to share my own story with her. I could not believe how open she was. I thought it was truly amazing that she could be so positive and take care of sick people in a dialysis center with a smile and an upbeat attitude after having overcome such adversity.

One Saturday, my wife was sitting with me during one of my treatments. I called over Tara and introduced them. In the middle of the conversation, I just blurted out to Tara, "What is your dream for your life?"

Instantly she responded and said, "I have always wanted to sing in a stadium…even if it was an empty stadium. That is my dream… to do that…once in my life."

A few weeks later I found a business card on my dialysis chair when I arrived for the day. A staff member thought that I might like to talk to her cousin who was a patient advocate from a transplant center. I struck up a friendship with the man who was also a former dialysis patient and kidney transplant recipient. I later found out that he was also active in raising awareness about organ donation. He asked for help selling tickets for a fundraiser at the New York Yankees' Triple-A baseball stadium in Scranton, Pennsylvania. I jumped at the opportunity, and soon after a light bulb went on in my head. *What if I asked my new friend if Tara could sing the national anthem that day?*

He informed me that, unfortunately, it was Yankee Legends Day at the stadium and former Yankees centerfielder Bernie Williams would be doing the national anthem on his guitar. I was not going to give up that easy. I asked my friend for the event contact and called and explained the situation. After some back and forth, the team agreed to let Tara sing "America the Beautiful" right before the national anthem that day.

When I got to the dialysis center the next day, I spoke privately with the charge nurse. I explained everything and asked permission to speak with Tara in the lobby to give her the good news. Tara was in shock and could not speak. That was the first time I ever saw her at a loss for words.

Two months later, everyone cheered as Tara's name was announced over the PA system as she appeared on the jumbotron screen at PNC Field at the opening of the Rail Riders game. It was super-hot that day, in the mid-90s. It was Organ Donation Awareness Day at the stadium. I was on the field enjoying every second of being a part of a dream fulfilled when Tara sang beautifully in front of 10,000 fans.

After she finished singing, Tara walked over to me behind home plate and gave me a big hug and whispered in my ear, "Thank you so much, Jay. I can't believe I just did that." I asked Bernie Williams if he would pose for a group photo with Tara and her boyfriend. Tara's smile told the whole story as she beamed for the photo.

Funny Business

I started doing standup comedy while I was teaching at an elementary school in upper Manhattan in the mid-1990s. This was comedy not just in the classroom, but as a stress release after school with my whacky friend Mike the Clown. He got me started and I met him on certain afternoons in the basement of the West End Bar near Columbia University for these open mics where no one laughed. It was brutal. I stood nervously in front of audiences comprised of other fledgling comedians. It was kind of harsh to not get much of a response, but it gave me a starting point to just get up to the microphone.

I also took a standup comedy class for six weeks, which culminated with a "graduation" performance on a real comedy club stage. Not long after, I performed at pre-shows at comedy clubs where it was required to bring at least three paying customers in exchange for a few minutes of stage time. I invited teachers whom I worked with to see me perform. I should have been embarrassed but I really enjoyed it. The principal of my school soon found out about these shows and posted little notices in the main office to let people know when I would be performing.

One day I was approached by the head janitor in the school named Pat. "Hey, Jay, do you want to go and see the Letterman show?"

I was puzzled but said, "Yeah, of course I do."

Now, Pat was an older Irish guy whom I had become friendly with, but I wondered how he could get me in to see the Letterman show. David Letterman had just moved over to CBS after ending his long tenure at NBC. The show was now broadcast from the Ed Sullivan Theater on Broadway and 53rd Street.

As it turned out, Pat's best friend Bill was a retired NYPD detective who had gone into security for television shows. Someone liked him at CBS and hired him to be David Letterman's bodyguard and head of security at the *Late Show*. Bill offered Pat a standing invitation to the show. Pat said, "Jay, I will never get down there with my schedule. Let me know when you want to go." So, I picked a date.

When I walked up and saw the marquee, "The Late Show with David Letterman," I felt so excited and hopeful that I would get in as planned. There was a long line of people wrapped around the block. I walked up to the front glass doors and a CBS usher cracked the door and asked what I wanted. "I'm here to see Bill." She told me to wait and after a minute Bill appeared in the doorway. He had a bushy mustache, wore an Armani suit, and spoke quickly and efficiently. Bill said, "You're Jay? Follow me." I tried hard to keep up with him as I followed him through the lobby and in through the inner doors leading into the studio. The theater was empty. He told me, "Sit here in the front row and watch the rehearsals. I'll be back."

A Broadway singer named Linda Eder rehearsed the song that she would perform during her segment with Paul Shaffer and the Late Show Band. Biff Henderson, the stage manager, buzzed around. I just could not believe I was there. How did I get there?

I sat there for a while and watched the rehearsals and pre-show sound checks. Bill came back before the public was let in and asked me, "Where do you want to sit for the show?" I said, "I will stay right here in the front row."

The following day at work, I thanked Pat and he told me, "I can get you in anytime. Just let me know." Pat had an inside scoop as to who the upcoming guests might be. This went on for a couple of years. I saw Don Rickles, Louie Anderson, George Carlin, and many more stars. I sometimes brought a friend with me to the show. I bought Pat and Bill bottles of champagne to thank them.

I noticed that there was this comedian named Eddie Brill who did the audience warm-up before each Letterman show. He seemed to be part of the Letterman "crew family" and was also very funny. One day after one of the shows, I saw him in the crowd as he exited the theater and approached him. I said, "Hey, Eddie, my name is Jay. I do a little standup."

He responded, "Nice to meet you, buddy. Why don't you come to a show I host every Monday at Caroline's." Caroline's was a well-known, upscale comedy club on 50th and Broadway. I could not believe that Eddie, an award-winning comedian, had asked me to come and be his guest at the show. Eddie told me, "On Monday nights Caroline's has their new talent come in."

I found out that a lot of up-and-coming comedians performed on that show to get a video of their act. Apparently, it was an industry standard for people who wanted to make an audition tape. The comedians who performed at Caroline's on Monday nights were already somewhat established comedians. This was not an open mic night or a preshow

That very next Monday I went downtown to Caroline's. I arrived an hour early and met Eddie down in the bar area outside of the showroom. He seemed excited and said, "There's someone here I want you to meet." I followed him into the showroom and he introduced me to the famous actor and comedian Dennis Leary, who was the celebrity guest that night on the show. The three of us stood and chatted near the stage of the empty club as the comedians who were performing that night started to arrive. It felt like a dream. How did I get there?

I stood in the hall and peeked inside the little dressing room located right across from their busy kitchen. I imagined all the stars who had been in there. I got so excited that I began to feel sick. Just then, a frenzied server tapped me on the shoulder. He said, "Do not get in the way of the wait staff once the showroom opens. They will knock you over." I wondered where to stand.

Suddenly, this guy came up to me and said, "Follow me to the back." I thought for a minute that I had done something wrong. "I'm Andy and I produce the New Talent Night shows. Eddie told me about you. I want to interview you to perform on a future show." I was caught off guard. We sat at a table in the empty club. I looked at the stage and lights as my stomach churned.

Andy asked, "How many sets do you do each week?"

I said, "Three or four usually."

He said, "Can you handle doing ten minutes of material?

I already felt a little sick and over-excited before this, but now I really started to feel ill. I felt myself becoming dizzy and nauseous.

As the audience was being seated, I met a comedian named John Bush. Some agents were there to look at him from a major network. I tried to get it together but I was overwhelmed and felt nauseous.

It was a sold-out show. My choices were to either stand and watch from the wings while I tried to avoid the wait staff as they bolted out of the kitchen or to listen from the dressing room. The roar of the laughter from the audience during John's set sent shivers up my spine, but I felt sicker and sicker. I did not want to leave, but it was getting worse.

John Bush saw me when he got off stage and said, "You look green," and directed me to the green room. I wondered if that was why the place where all the nervous performers went was called the green room. Once inside the bathroom, I vomited repeatedly. John said, "I will walk you up and get you a taxi." As I left the showroom, I said a quick goodbye to Dennis Leary and Eddie, who were puzzled as to why I was leaving in such a hurry.

John walked me through the bar area. Just as we reached the foot of the stairs, an agent walked up and said, "John, that was great—we'd like to talk to you." John gave me a quick sympathetic nod and walked off with the agent.

I went up the stairs and got a taxi. I knew that I would not make it home, so I asked the driver to bring me to the hospital where I stayed for three hours with an IV for dehydration until I gradually started to feel better. I found out later John Bush clinched a deal with a major network from that night's performance. Not long after, I saw him appear on his own Comedy Central special and on several sitcom episodes.

I got a call from Andy a few days later. He said, "We have an opening for you to perform at an upcoming New Talent Night at Caroline's in three months." I was stunned for a moment before Andy said, "Are you interested in performing for ten minutes?"

I said, "Yes!"

"All you have to do is invite your friends and family. Let me know if you want a video of your performance."

So, the date was set for October 20, 1997. I could not believe it. Ten minutes seemed like a long time up there in front of an audience. At that point, I had only done open mics and pre-shows. I wanted to be prepared. Over the next few months, I went to clubs and brought guests to get stage time. I performed at the Gotham Comedy Club and Standup New York to see what worked in my routine. Since I was a heavy guy with a belly, I created a routine in which I was a retired Chippendales dancer. I made up a lot of weight jokes and added a few minutes of funny personal and stock jokes.

Sure enough, there was a teacher at my school who asked me for a favor. Apparently, she had a daughter who was getting married and they were having a bridal shower and wanted to hire me as a comedian for $50. It was ridiculous as I did not have the experience and initially said no. Then I thought about my future performance at Caroline's and reconsidered. I needed something like this to break through my fear before the big show and agreed to do it.

I later found out that the daughter's friend was hosting the event. She was very wealthy and lived in a penthouse on Sutton Place in Manhattan. Her father was the CEO of Snapple. I should not have accepted the invitation or been involved but clung to the idea that it would be good preparation for me the day before I would hit the stage at Caroline's Comedy Club.

When I arrived at the Sutton Place penthouse, I was ushered into a bedroom and told to wait until after the cocktail hour. I could hear the clinking of glasses in the other room as they toasted the bride. I was sweating profusely and felt like I wanted to leave or rather escape and almost did. Suddenly, the mother of the bride appeared and brought me out to the party room.

There were a lot of very rich people there, but mostly Jewish women in their forties and fifties. The bartender flashed me a concerned look from across the room. The place was beautiful with big floor-to-ceiling windows and panoramic views of the city. Butlers were serving drinks from a full bar.

Once I saw my audience, I knew there was no way they should have had a comedian here, and certainly not me. They had started my entrance song, "It's Raining Men," a little late so it was still playing as I stood there frozen in front of the room. As I started my routine about how I used to work at Chippendales, I could already tell that they were ignoring me.

I said, "If you don't laugh, I'll start stripping." I removed my blazer and then started unbuttoning my dress shirt. Women started to scream but in horror. I went up to one of the older women and said, "I know you want it."

In the entire group, there was only one woman there, maybe in her twenties, who thought that I was funny. This whole thing took place the day before I was supposed to perform at Caroline's and I thought that if I could do this in front of all these older women, I could do anything. The bride's mother stuck a $50 bill in my pants and escorted me out. My future wife Ellen was waiting outside in her car and we took off.

The next day, I took the subway to Caroline's for my big performance. I had sent out postcard invitations to everyone I knew and hoped that people called in to make their reservations.

It was October so it was already dark by the time that I got off the subway at Columbus Circle and walked into the cold air and darkness. Nobody was around on the streets at that time of night. I walked briskly and thought about whether I could do this performance. I noticed someone was walking toward me, bundled up with a scarf and hat on. It was a wide sidewalk so I found it weird that the person who approached was walking kind of close to me. The person looked at me and purposely veered in my direction. We were on a collision course. Just then, as I tried to walk around, her arm reached out and grabbed my arm. Out of all the people in New York City, it was that one woman who had laughed at my jokes at the bridal shower the day before. She had recognized me and said, "I thought you were really funny yesterday. I loved it." It was just what I needed.

I got to the club early and sat on the side of the bar with an eagle-eye view of the hostess stand. More and more people I knew walked in to check in with the hostess. I was astonished when I found out that sixty-eight people had shown up for me. Most comedians had five or ten guests. I appreciated the support and it lifted my confidence level. Even my therapist surprised me and came out to see me perform.

Eddie Brill hosted the show and I was the second to last performer in the lineup out of eight comedians.

I thought back to the last time I was there and how sick I was. To my surprise, I bumped into John Bush outside of the dressing room and he could not believe I was there to perform. John was there to support a comedian friend named Nick from his hometown in Minnesota. Nick was a young prodigy only seventeen or eighteen years old. It was his first time in New York City and he also had agents there to see him. Nick and I stood in front of the mirror in the dressing room together. Nick was the cleanup act right after me.

He asked me, "Are you nervous?"

I said, "No. I just don't want to fall on the way up to the stage."

He said, "Then why are you tightening your belt so much?"

"I want to seem as fat as possible for my routine," I said.

He looked nervous. His name was Nick Swardson. He later became famous and appeared on several television shows and in movies and eventually toured worldwide.

I felt confident and excited. It was warm and bright on the stage and I could only make out a few faces in the front. When I said my first line, people laughed. It was such a high to hear that response, and my body was tingling all over and I wanted more laughter. I messed up one line, but I improvised something out of it. Everything was a blur once I handed the microphone back to Eddie. I could not believe all the people were there and that they laughed.

At the end, a comedian and some other guys asked me if I wanted to go out for a drink. My head was still spinning and my whole body was vibrating. We went to the Marriott Marquis Time Bar and I was just basking in the whole thing. All the things I had gone through just to be there. I could not sleep that whole night and the next day I felt like I was floating while I was walking to school in the morning. I was just on a different level.

A week or so after my Caroline's debut, I stood outside of the Ed Sullivan Theater as I waited to meet a friend. I saw Eddie Brill walking across the street on his way into work but did not want to bother him. He turned and saw me at the last second before he went through the front door of the theater, then came over to shake my hand. He turned to me and said, "You did a good job the other night." That was an awesome life moment for me. People were standing there probably wondering how I knew him.

Later that night, I went to pick up my Caroline's performance video from a studio on 57th Street. When I entered the video office there was an older black man talking to the editor. He turned around. It was Nipsey Russell, the famous comedian and poet. I recognized him immediately, rushed toward him, and spontaneously hugged him.

Without hesitation, I said, "I just performed at Caroline's. Will you watch my tape with me and let me know what you think?"

He said, "Okay, kid."

The room had a tiny monitor and one folding chair. He sat down and I hunched over and together we watched my performance for the first time.

Nipsey said, "What do you do for a living?"

I said, "I'm a schoolteacher."

"That's a good profession," said Nipsey. "You are used to being up in front of an audience."

"So, what do you think?" I asked.

Nipsey said, "You are comfortable in front of an audience and that makes sense because you are a teacher. You're funny and have potential."

* * *

I did not really believe that I was going to have a career as a comedian, but I loved the behind-the-scenes stuff. I wanted to produce my own professional standup comedy shows. I started going to different NYC comedy clubs looking for the funniest people that

I could find. When I saw someone I liked, I waited in the lobby and approached them and asked them to be in one of my shows. Invariably, they would ask me, "Who are you?" I would always start by telling them that I knew Eddie Brill from the Letterman show and Eddie would vouch for me.

I found small theaters on 44th Street between 8th and 9th Avenues in this place called The Producers Club. It happened to be located right upstairs from the original famous Improv, founded in 1963 by Bud Friedman, which was now an Italian restaurant. They even saved part of the original brick wall from The Improv. I decided to rent out the theater upstairs and get the best NYC comedians for each show. I traveled around the city to make relationships with hotels and other places to promote my shows. Eddie Brill performed a set on my first show. It was a dream come true for me.

I got to book and hang out with comedians like Jim Gaffigan. I saw him for the first time in 1996 and loved him and thought he was very funny. In 1998 I told Jim how unbelievable it was that he was not on a sitcom and predicted his career path. Jim told me, "It's not that easy, Jay." He did eight shows with me at The Producers Club. Eddie Brill went on to become entertainment coordinator for the Letterman show and booked all the comedians for the show. Eight months later Gaffigan got booked on *The Late Show* and was signed that same night by David Letterman's Worldwide Pants Production Company.

I knew that I wanted to be involved with performers and to bring audiences together. I wanted to be involved as a manager and producer, but I also wanted there to be an educational point to it. I decided to merge the performance aspect with my background in education. I founded a speakers bureau, which provided motivational and inspirational presenters for schools, colleges, and other organizations on a variety of topics. This was the beginning of A Vision in Motion Speakers Bureau.

* * *

I had all of the old home numbers of all the comedians I'd booked in the 1990s. Many of them had become super successful in movies and television. Some had become writers and producers for major shows while others toured the world. People had cell numbers now, but I was able to get in touch with Eddie Brill for my Reconnection Tour because he had kept his home number connected just in case. Eddie helped change the trajectory of my life after I met him at the Letterman show. We met up twice on my Reconnection Tour. First, we got together at a café in New York City, and one night my daughter and I met up with him for a Mets game at Citi Field. We are both big Mets fans.

I thanked Eddie for all he had done in helping me make my comedy performing and producing dreams come true. He said, "Jay, I helped you out a little, but you are the one who made it happen! It is because of the person you are. Don't forget that."

Bill, The Blessed Gambler

When I first went back to New York at age nineteen, I saw a sign that read "Bus to Atlantic City." I was very curious so one cloudy, cold day, miserably lonely and just bored out of my mind, I decided to hop on a bus to south Jersey. When I finally arrived and stepped off the bus it was dusk. I looked at the bright, colorful lights lining the buildings and streets and felt inspired and mesmerized.

As I entered one of the casinos, the sounds, the flashing lights, and the crowds of people talking and shouting made me happy and excited. I did not have a lot of money and I did not know how to gamble. It was just something about the sense of adventure that attracted me. I remember seeing a poster there saying, "If you think you have a gambling problem, call this number." It was for Gambler's Anonymous (GA). Even though I did not have a gambling problem I called the number. The guy on the phone told me about a twelve-step program. I decided to go to a meeting.

The meeting was in the basement of a small church. There were about ten people there and everybody introduced themselves. I enjoyed the meeting, hearing the different stories and issues people were having, and I participated a little. After the meeting people were having refreshments and talking. A guy named Mark came up to me and said we had a lot in common and said he should be my sponsor. I thought it was amazing to have someone who cared and wanted to talk to me.

I started going to the meeting every week. This guy Mark was in his forties and took me under his wing, and I met his family and would sometimes go to his house. The people in the program would tell me that I was not addicted to gambling but I wanted to belong so I did not leave. I was not gambling but I was becoming friends with a lot of people. I became really close with Mark, my "sponsor," and he would invite me to his vacation home with his family and it was amazing. The people in the meetings would ask me questions about my gambling and I really did not qualify.

I decided to go to a different meeting on a Sunday. As I entered the room, I noticed the people there seemed worse off than the ones who came to the Saturday meeting. They were poorer and were in some deep trouble due to their addiction. A lot of people there were very sick and I listened to some of their very sad stories. There was all this gambling terminology and a lot of people who had lost their things and lives and families to gambling. This is where I met Bill K.

Bill looked a little disheveled and kind of like a fish out of water. He had white curly hair and wore a gray hat, sneakers, brown corduroy pants that seemed too large for him, and a dark blue jacket that seemed a bit faded and worn. He must have been in his sixties. He did not seem comfortable there. At the end of the meeting, I felt an urge to share my thoughts. Bill stared at first and then his eyes seemed to light up. He was holding a cane and wobbled over to me and introduced himself. It was an instant connection.

Bill immediately started telling me about his life. He said his family came from Ireland and he had worked as a professional waiter on the *Queen Elizabeth II* for almost twenty years. He served mostly royalty on fancy ships. Eventually he had enough of ships and decided to get a job at the Plaza Hotel in NYC. He spent the next twenty years as a server there with a butler's outfit for the rich and famous. Eventually he was promoted to head room service waiter at the Plaza. He interacted with rich and famous celebrities, dignitaries, countless professional athletes, actors, singers, even some kings and princes, all staying in the fanciest Plaza suites.

His wife worked as a live-in nanny for the rich and famous in Greenwich, Connecticut. He had a lot of amazing stories to tell. I found all this very fascinating and enjoyed listening to his stories. I was shocked to hear that he was forced to retire early since he had suddenly found he was developing Parkinson's disease and started freezing up and not being able to work anymore. He was totally destroyed since his whole life had been this job, which he enjoyed every minute of, and now he was stuck with serious physical challenges and nothing to do every day. So here was this guy who was rubbing elbows with all these great personalities, having the time of his life, making a good living, and suddenly it was all cruelly ripped away from him by this insidious disease. That is how he ended up addicted to gambling.

Bill started gambling after he lost his job, and then his wife left him when he dropped all his money into slot machines after he was diagnosed with Parkinson's. Bill was so funny and amazing and I tried to become friends with him. I would go to certain meetings that he would attend. People always tried to help him and he would always go back to the gambling. He didn't have any money and he became homeless. He eventually ended up in a homeless shelter, but I stayed in touch with him through the meetings. I wished that he was normal and I could just have a normal relationship with him, but he was sick and he couldn't get it together.

When I first met Bill I lived in an apartment in upper Manhattan and was teaching at an elementary school in that same neighborhood. He was very funny and knew a lot of jokes because of all the years on the cruise ship. This was before I met my wife, and I was doing standup comedy at the time. I asked Bill to come see my act and maybe help write me some jokes. He would always try to get me to take a bus with him to Atlantic City when he would get his monthly disability check. Sometimes I would go with him just so I could talk to him on the way down. I just wanted to spend time with him. That was not the GA way, but I was lonely and it was my only way to sometimes get to spend some time with him.

One day I got a call on a Friday morning from Bill as I was just getting ready to start Spring Break. He was saying goodbye and told me he was going to Atlantic City and was not coming back. I thought that was going to be it, since he had threatened to end it all one day. I could not let it go. I loved him so much and wanted to save him. I was feeling kind of sick to my stomach that day but rented a car and drove down to Atlantic City. I went to his usual hotel and to the front desk and lied, saying that my uncle was there and they gave me the room number. I ran all the way to his room and started knocking on the door and calling his name. I was overwhelmed, felt nervous, and began to feel sick.

He was not responding and I was standing there sweating for a very long time and was getting scared. A couple of people opened their doors, peeking out to see what was going on. I was getting ready to get management to open the door when I suddenly heard some rustling around in there. Many times before he would just freeze up because of his Parkinson's, so I was hoping he was trying to get to the door. I finally heard "hold on" and was instantly relieved.

He finally opened the door and was pissed because it was hard for him to maneuver and I do not think he wanted me to come down there at all. I told him I was so worried after that message he left. I was still nervous and kind of nauseous, so I went to the bathroom in his room and had the runs. I was sitting on the toilet for like thirty minutes and he told me he would go down to the gift shop and get me some Pepto-Bismol to settle my stomach. I gave him $20. He took the money, but never came back. I finally got off the toilet, paged him, but he never responded.

I looked everywhere in the casino and two other surrounding casinos for about two hours. I went back to his room, but the door was locked and he was not answering this time. I found the manager and told him I was worried about "Uncle Bill" so he opened the door for me. The only things I found in there were his wallet, passport, and other personal belongings. It was just so odd and bizarre that he would just disappear on me like that and leave all his personal belongings behind. I decided to take his things and go out again to try and find him. I was scared he might have gone to the pier and jumped. He always threatened that one day if things got too bad, he would jump into the ocean. I thought he just wanted to get away from me so he could do just that; why else would he leave all his stuff behind?

Worried and frustrated, I walked around for hours searching for him. I finally decided to go to the police station. The cop at the front desk said that they hear stuff like this all the time and told me I could not file a missing person report yet. He said they would send a detective over to the hotel to investigate. I left all his personal belongings with the police department. They said they would be in touch. I was feeling so sick as I drove all the way back to New York City to my apartment. Anything I tried to eat or drink was coming up; I just could not stop barfing. My eyes were bloody. The blood vessels in my eyes had burst from all the heaving. Luckily, it was still spring break so I did not have to go in to teach for another week.

I did not hear anything all weekend, and five days later I got a call and it was from Bill. He wanted to know why I took off with his ID. I asked him why he never came back after hours and told him I was looking for him. He was pissed because all of his stuff was in Atlantic City and he had to wait to have everything mailed back to him, but I was pissed off too because he had left me like that and scared the shit out of me. It took a long time for us to talk again. After that it was difficult to deal with him. I stayed in touch with him a little but it was not the same after that.

Eventually Bill got a small apartment on the Lower East Side in an assisted living building. I would visit him once in a while and buy him groceries, but not give him money since I knew he would just gamble it away. During that time, I had gotten married and moved to New Jersey. I introduced him to my wife and we would both go to the city to see him and take him out to dinner. There was a garden in his building and Bill was really into gardening, but he had to do it from his motorized wheelchair since he could not walk anymore. His Parkinson's meds had stopped working.

When Bill was a room service waiter he had a writing pad and when he would go around taking orders, he would have famous people sign the pad and keep the autographs for his collection. He had all these stories about famous people that he had met. But now Bill had a different pad. In the garden, he started writing poetry and ended up becoming a poet. He also started taking art classes and painting. He was gifted and it was his therapy. I am lucky to have something to share that he created.

It is a poem called "The Garden."

On a street of many sounds
Stands a garden where peace abounds
The morning dew flows over the leaves like satin
It's hard to believe you're in Manhattan

You can bear the silence, but not for long
For soon the birds burst into song
They act as if they are very late
Maybe they have a heavy date

The rain brings the magic and the splendor
Showing off the flowers in all this grandeur
Soon the garden will be in full bloom
Despite the outside stress and doom

If life is unkind put it out of your mind
Sit and relax far away from the fax
Look up at the sky and you will see why
When God made Heaven
He left a little behind

By Bill K.

Over time Bill became an avid painter and spent most of his time creating new paintings. Bill had a doctor in Queens and every time he had an appointment he brought him one of his paintings. The doctor loved his paintings and started buying them from Bill. One day I went with Bill to Queens and met the doctor and the walls were all covered with Bill's paintings. It was like a museum of his work. We took photos of them all.

I continued to see Bill periodically over the next few years but not very often as my wife and I got busier raising our daughter Lizzie. I also had my own business by that time. But we would sometimes pick a Saturday or Sunday to go with Lizzie to the city and we would visit Bill. His apartment was very small, so we would sometimes sit in the garden, or take him out for coffee and something to eat. He would always try and trick me into going gambling with him, but I told him I was just not into that anymore. Every time we visited he gave us one of his paintings to take home. Unfortunately, he was still addicted to gambling and tended to run out of food. He admitted he still gambled when he got his disability check and lost it all. I would still buy him groceries.

When I was planning my thirtieth birthday party I convinced Bill to come. I picked him up and brought him to my home in Rutherford, New Jersey. Bill flirted with one of my guests, a teacher from the school I used to teach in, and it seemed like he had a good time. It meant a lot to me that he was there. I somehow lost touch with him for a while after that. I tried to call him, but his phone was disconnected. When I called the building management they said he was no longer a resident there. I called some people I knew from the meetings and they said they had not seen him. One day in 2004 I got a call from a guy I knew from one of the Gamblers Anonymous meetings where they gave Bill coffee and donuts. He gave me the bad news that Bill was gone. Apparently, he had taken one last trip to Atlantic City and drove his wheelchair off the pier.

I couldn't find any more information about what had happened, any of his family members, or any obituaries or funeral information. This was not surprising since Bill had been abandoned and disowned long ago by his family, and although he had made many overtures to his ex-wife over the years, she was so devastated by Bill's gambling addiction and behavior that she could never reconcile with him. The loss of his wife actually made his condition worse.

I could never forget Bill and I reminisce about him periodically. I remember all the smart advice he used to give me on many topics. He was like a father figure. Bill would always tell me to have confidence. "When you walk in a place, act like you own it." Bill was my first comedy coach when I first took a standup comedy class and attended my "graduation" show at Stand Up New York. I used some of his stock jokes from the cruise ships. I remember when I met a girl for dinner whom I had not seen in many years. Bill told me to get a bite to eat beforehand "to take the edge off."

One time I just really wanted to be with Bill and he just wanted to go to Atlantic City. I met him at the Port Authority and bought two tickets. We talked until the bus was ready to leave the station.

I decided not to go. He went without me. It was enough for me to have had a little time with him. I don't think he cared either way. He just wanted that ticket to Atlantic City. Bill would do anything to make a few dollars and then gamble it away.

Someone approached him to pose naked in a book for an artist doing a book about a cross-section of naked people in New York City. He did it and the book was published and he was proud of it. Bill wanted a word processor to do his poetry. I gave him an all-in-one word processor that I had used all through college. When I visited him I noticed it was missing. Bill had sold it and gambled the money away.

People loved Bill for his quick sense of humor in his Irish brogue. He was sharp and observant and cared for others. His sickness led him down a very dark path. As his illness worsened and worsened, his medications worked less and less. Bill sold one of his motorized wheelchairs that he had gotten through disability and gambled the proceeds. Somehow, he always seemed to get another one. When he was without it, he would try to walk across a busy NYC street and freeze up right in the middle of the street with horns honking and people screaming at him. He was a tortured soul, but he managed to still give the world his best when he was not gambling.

What's Happening!!

I grew up in the 1970s and enjoyed watching television sitcoms. My favorite actor from a show called *What's Happening!!* was Fred Berry, who played "Rerun." He was the heavyset, loveable, high-energy character on the show who always wore a red beret and suspenders. Rerun could bring down the house with his surprisingly athletic dancing. Since I was also the chubby or fat kid, he was someone I really got a kick out of seeing show off on television. I was lonely a lot after school. Food was my best friend but that kept me the fat kid, which did not help my social life. My popular older brother had many friends and I always tried to convince him to let me tag along.

I knew somewhere deep inside there was something special for me to do in the world. I vividly remember sitting alone under a huge oak tree crying and repeating to myself, "I could be something one day. Why am I so alone and why doesn't anyone see me?" Daydreams had become more like visions and sometimes flash in my mind. I could sometimes picture myself in the future doing something important or maybe standing in front of an audience. At about ten years old I had already made a plan that I would become a sports and entertainment lawyer. Then, I would be able to get close to famous athletes and celebrities and be on the inside of that television.

I was a top student in school and sort of like a "brain." I felt as if my gifted and talented teacher in the fifth grade, Mrs. Lustberg, somehow saw something in me and had a vision for me as well. She wrote a special message in my 1981 memory book, which I saved.

Dear Jay,

Once in a while teachers have a special feeling for a student and a unique relationship. I'm so happy we had the opportunity to share many wonderful experiences together! I know it won't end here—I'll be sharing your future!"

Love, Mrs. Lustberg

My life's path could have and maybe should have been much easier. I did not make it to law school to become an entertainment lawyer. However, the universe aligned so that somehow later in life I was reunited on a meaningful personal level with some of the sports and entertainment figures with whom I felt special connections.

* * *

Twenty years after watching Rerun dance and dazzle on the television show *What's Happening!!*, our paths crossed in 1998 when I met Fred "Rerun" Berry at the New York Comedy Club's '70s Throwback Night. I was leaving the club and saw him sitting alone at a table so I introduced myself. He invited me to pull up a chair and we started talking. I explained to him that I was a teacher and that I had also produced standup comedy shows at a small theater called The Producers Club with top New York City talent. I gave him my business card.

The next day Fred called me. He said that he wanted to perform in my next standup comedy showcase. I told him that I did not have a large budget and was not sure if I could afford him. "Jay,

I would love to be a part of the show and if I can sell autographs, I'm cool." I agreed and thought Fred, who told me he had legally changed his name to Rerun, would be quite an attraction as he was so recognizable and the audience would get a kick out of seeing him. I was a little surprised when Fred invited me to meet up with him beforehand. He said, "I want to get to know each other and tell you my story." He gave me his address and we made an appointment to get together the next Friday afternoon after work.

I took the subway downtown to 34th Street and walked a few long blocks west and found his building. Fred had told me to ring the bell for the penthouse. It was not a super fancy building and I was a bit nervous when I was buzzed into the front door. When I stepped off the elevator at the penthouse floor, I was welcomed by Fred and saw him in the light for the first time since that meeting in the dark club. I was surprised to see how much thinner he was now in his late forties.

We walked into the apartment and Fred explained that it belonged to a music producer whom he had befriended as a struggling wannabe in the 1970s in Hollywood when Rerun was at the height of his television show success, making millions. We walked into the office/guest room that the music producer had provided for him now that he was broke. I saw a full-on recording studio and an expansive series of rooms and a great view of the city through glass windows on the opposite side of the hallway.

Fred began to tell me the story of his life, which started with his humble beginnings in an inner-city housing project in St. Louis. He talked about being a member of the Locker Dancers in the early '70s and about his time on the TV dance show *Soul Train*. I was sad to learn of how he had struggled with drug and alcohol addiction. Fred explained that he had spent money extravagantly on a Leer jet and horses. He explained that he had lined up a deal with a toy company to mass-market his TV character likeness, but that a dispute over rights with the network negated the deal. Fred described a meeting in a conference room with the group of all-white TV network executives. He was so enraged by what he felt was their racist treatment that he stood up and walked out after unloading some choice words on them. I believe this was the reason that Rerun parted ways with the reunion show of *What's Happening Now!!*.

Fred explained to me that he had found the Lord and became a minister speaking at churches. He had also started the "Rerun Dance and Acting School" in New York City where he coached and trained up-and-coming actors and dancers. I listened intently and Fred seemed very comfortable with me. We went up to the roof and looked out over the city and talked some more about Fred making an appearance on my next comedy showcase.

A few weeks later I sat with Fred in the small dressing room of the theater that I had rented for my standup comedy showcase. I felt proud to be there with him. He performed his comedy routine dressed in drag as "Moms Mabley" who was a well-known African American female vaudeville comedian. It was not that funny a bit, but a long line formed in the reception area as people were eager to get Rerun's autograph for five bucks after the show.

Fred called me again to ask if I could return to the penthouse to meet his music producer friend, who wanted my thoughts on how to get Rerun back in the spotlight and jumpstart his career. I took it seriously and asked my writer friend, Chris, to accompany me. It was a real meeting and I shared my thoughts about Fred doing a one-man show about his life. I hated to think about Fred "Rerun" Berry as a has-been. I wondered if my childhood visions had anything to do with how I ended up in a room encouraging the man who had encouraged me as a kid on the inside of that television.

Carlin at Carnegie

My mother decided to go back to graduate school when I was in elementary school. After finishing her master's in teaching English as a Second Language, she decided to go on for her doctorate at Teachers College, Columbia University. So, in 1981 my father, mother, brother, and I, as well as a crazy little dog named Champ, moved out of a large, rented house in Paramus, New Jersey and into this cramped, two-bedroom apartment in Morningside Heights at 509 W. 121st Street. We lived in a New York City landmark building called Bancroft Hall that was housing for married graduate students attending Teachers College. We were one of the few American families who lived in the building. There were families from all over the world who traveled there so that a parent could study at this prestigious learning institution.

The window of my world opened wide. I started to learn about other cultures firsthand. I always said that from eleven to fourteen years old I went to graduate school with my mother. I lived her Ivy League experience. I met a lot of famous professors, went to cultural events on campus, and heard world-renowned speakers and authors. I used the Teachers College library for my school research projects and imagined one day going to law school or earning a doctorate myself. Basically, I absorbed the intellectual and cultural fumes around Columbia.

Numerous iconic cultural, religious, and educational institutions with rich history were all over the neighborhood. We lived right across the street from Teacher's College. The skyscraper towering up the block was Riverside Church, which is one of New York's most prominent religious landmarks. Just across the street from there was Grant's Tomb in Riverside Park. The Union Theological Seminary was a block away, with the Jewish Theological Seminary down the block on Broadway. At 112th Street was the Cathedral of St. John the Divine, the largest Gothic cathedral in the world. Columbia University's main campus and Barnard were a stone's throw away at 116th Street.

Being a child of a student at Teachers College came with some perks. I had a family pass to the gymnasium on Columbia's main campus where I played basketball on a regular basis. Even as a thirteen-year-old in 1983, I had conversations with Columbia undergrads at the gym who spoke with me about applying to top law schools, like a senior named Barack Obama who planned to go to Harvard. I took a mock trial course for gifted kids through Columbia and won my case as the prosecuting attorney. Teacher's College had a student activities department and so we could get discount tickets for concerts, the opera, and different events including Broadway shows. It was really an amazing experience, and living in New York City opened my window to the world.

One event that we went to stemmed from my parents having liked the comedian George Carlin back in the 1960s. Tickets were available for "Carlin at Carnegie" in 1983. The legendary comedian had just recovered from a heart attack and a cocaine problem and was making his comeback performance at Carnegie Hall. Although I did not know who he was, my parents had been fans of his and said we should go and see the "hippy dippy weatherman." I am not exactly sure how appropriate it was to bring young teenaged kids to a George Carlin show, but we went to Carnegie Hall to hear him do his comeback performance. I do not remember exactly how much I understood of his material, but it was just exciting to be there. I noticed people were walking out toward the end of his performance and I could tell it was not like his best show ever. My parents were saying that it was unusual that people were leaving early, but it was an experience to say you had been to see George Carlin that Saturday night.

The next morning, I went out to walk the dog. There was a big courtyard outside our building at 509 W. 121st St. Just as I stepped out onto the sidewalk with Champ, I saw a long, black limousine pull up in front of me. I was surprised as I had not seen very many limousines in that neighborhood. I was curious as to who was inside. The door opened and almost in a dream sequence it was George Carlin! Now we had just been to see him at Carnegie Hall the night before on that interesting little escapade with my parents and suddenly there he was getting out of the limousine. I knew I had just seen him the night before on stage. I could not believe it.

I ran upstairs with the dog. I said, "You're not gonna believe this—a limousine just pulled up and George Carlin just got out." They did not believe me. So, my brother went downstairs with me to confirm my sighting. A film crew was already setting up. George Carlin had come with a video crew to film a documentary about his experience as a kid growing up on this street! What an unbelievable thing. George Carlin had come back to the block where he had spent his childhood, including where he went to school at the Corpus Christie Church right at the end of the street. In his youth it was predominantly an Irish/Jewish area. He grew up in the "Miami" building at 519 W. 121 St., which was right next door to where I lived.

He was there with his daughter and his wife and a camera crew, and he spent the whole day on the block. Carlin filmed scenes and talked about his life. We spoke to him and he thought it was amazing that two kids from 121st Street were at Carnegie Hall the night before and heard him in concert. I took some pictures with him and spoke to him in between his video shoot segments. I thought it was really one of those amazing things to have had this experience, and years later, getting involved in comedy and producing shows, and having had an experience like that.

Carlin performed relentlessly all over the country at any venue he could. Almost every night of the week he performed somewhere around the country. My wife and I went to some concert venue in New Jersey to see him in the late '90s. I had written a letter to him, paid the usher $10 if he would bring it backstage about my connection to him and meeting him and how I was involved in doing standup and producing my own shows. It was just another little connection to someone that was beyond just meeting the person.

Recently, I was reading his book that he had worked on for many years, which is called *Last Words*, which was published posthumously. There is a description about him growing up in that neighborhood and it was a perfect description that matched my impression of the neighborhood forty years after he lived there.

The Cool School

After the fifth grade when we moved to New York City I aced the "ERBs," which were the private school entrance placement tests, but my parents did not have enough money to send both my brother and me to private schools. I went to a public intermediate school called IS 44 on 77th Street diagonally across from the Museum of Natural History on the Upper West Side off Columbus Avenue. I had some great teachers there.

Especially amazing was my English teacher, Mr. Thatcher, who was in his late forties, always wore black, and taught Shakespeare and poetry like it was a college-level literature review. He was quite an intimidating intellectual force in the room and probably the best teacher I ever had in my life.

However, I still wanted to do what my brother was doing and was envious that he got to go to a small private prep school called McBurney School located on 63rd Street between Broadway and Central Park West. It was a school of kids mostly into the arts and sports. It was an eclectic mix of kids. There were musicians, actors, kids of celebrities, and burnouts. McBurney had a cool feel to it. Whenever there was a school play or an event at McBurney I would go and just think that I wanted to be there too. After my sixth-grade year at IS 44 my parents made some sort of financial aid deal to let me go there. McBurney was really my brother's school and I just wanted to experience what he did. I always seemed to be left behind.

Some of the students at McBurney were child actors shooting commercials or feature films. It even included a few musicians who spent half the day at Julliard across the street at Lincoln Center. These kids still wanted to experience real school while pursuing careers in entertainment. It was not unusual for someone to make a movie like an older kid named Rusty Jacobs. He acted in a movie with former McBurney student Robert De Niro and played young Deniro's character in the epic movie *Once Upon a Time in America*. These young actors returned to school without fanfare and played on sports teams like everyone else. Many parents at this school were famous commentators, journalists, and writers who worked on television shows like *Saturday Night Live* or on Broadway in every possible capacity you could think of.

One kid a few years older than me named Adam Horovitz, whom I saw in a McBurney school play by ancient Greek playwright Aristophanes called *The Birds*, later dropped out of school to join a musical group called the Beastie Boys. His father was a famous playwright named Israel Horovitz.

McBurney's famous alumni included such actors as Richard Thomas ("John Boy" from *The Waltons*) and Henry Winkler ("The Fonz" from *Happy Days*) as well as TV journalist Ted Koppel (*Nightline*), to mention just a few. Even J.D. Salinger, author of *The Catcher in The Rye*, had attended McBurney for two years.

I started the seventh grade at McBurney. I met a tall, gangly, annoying kid with blond hair named Michael Rappaport. He was a real wise guy who would constantly interrupt the teachers. The dean of the middle school, who doubled as the social studies teacher, was a very proud, regal man named Mr. Barnes. He walked with a cane and severe limp from being stabbed in an attempted mugging years before, and everyone respected him. When Michael would act up by blocking my hand when I raised it to answer a question, Mr. Barnes would take a tennis ball out of his desk and whip it across the room at Michael. It was his form of discipline. I did try out for the eighth grade basketball team and I made it! I played with Rappaport on that team.

Years later, Michael went on to become a television and movie star. I was in the early stages of my Reconnection Tour and already six months on dialysis when I met up with Michael Rappaport at his book signing in October 2017. Michael said, "I remember you" before he signed my book and grabbed my phone so that we could take a selfie video together on my phone. I forgot to hit record so we had to try again. Michael said, "McBurney alums part two, take two with Jay Gittleson. We're in Ridgewood, New Jersey out here at the big book signing." As three people lingered on the side waiting for an autograph, he added, "The crowd is too big—we didn't want to show it." I mentioned briefly that I was on dialysis. Michael said, "Good to see you, my man. Stay focused and take care of business."

Thinking back on my McBurney days, I can remember feeling so alone at lunchtime. I would sit by myself in the "commons" cafeteria area and eat my lunch and then I would look for a place to hide. The school shared the building with the YMCA and there was a pool that you had to walk through to get to the locker rooms for gym class. I would walk up to the balcony over the pool and sit there to kill time. Occasionally a student would walk through on their way to the locker rooms. A few people might have said "Are you ok?" or something but for the most part I just wanted the time to go by until the next class started. I was just so scared inside and did not really have that "coolness" to feel like I fit in with the other kids.

Even though I was on the outside looking in at these interesting people as they passed me on the pool balcony or in the hallways and stairwells of this tiny private school, I loved being close to the action and making note of what students or their siblings at McBurney were doing. I knew many of their names and their backstories just by listening, observing, even sometimes looking them up in the yearbook. I knew that fellow student Stephanie Givens had an older sister named Robin Givens, who was a model and actress. Robin later married heavyweight champion Mike Tyson. Another upperclassman named Patrick Sheedy had an older sister named Allie who had starred in several movies during that time period including *WarGames*, *Oxford Blues*, and *The Breakfast Club*. There was an attractive senior named Tasia Valenza who had a role on the soap opera *All my Children* and starred in a movie called *Crackers* while she was a fellow student at McBurney.

I later followed the careers of the people I went to school with at McBurney. Adam Horovitz and the Beastie Boys were inducted into the Rock and Roll Hall of Fame in 2012 with a special introduction from LL Cool Jay. In fact, Beastie Boys group member Adam Horovitz, aka "Adrock," had discovered LL Cool Jay's demo tape in Def Jam Founder Rick Rubin's dorm room at NYU while a student at McBurney. Adam had urged Rubin, who was flooded with demos, to listen to then fourteen-year-old LL's tape.

I spoke to LL Cool Jay in 2013 at the Riverside Square Mall at Bloomingdale's, where his wife was introducing a new line of jewelry that she had designed. I told him that I had gone to school with Adam Horovitz during the time period that Adam had discovered him. LL Cool Jay hugged me tightly and it felt special in that moment as his bodyguards retreated to give me that space. My eleven-year-old daughter took our photo.

Follow the Bouncing Ball

I woke up gasping for air as I ripped off my breathing mask with my CPAP machine whistling away as the air escaped. The television was still on as my eyes struggled to focus on the screen in front of me. The camera zoomed in closer and closer on a black and white photo of my teenaged self. I thought maybe it was a dream in progress and I was still sleeping. The camera panned to the photo next to mine. I finally understood that I was watching the nightly news and that the focus of the story was directed at my former 1988 Teaneck High School classmate, Lawrence Frank.

My yearbook photo had landed right between two future professional sports figures. To my right was Doug Glanville, an early childhood friend, who went on to become a professional baseball player after being drafted in the first round by the Chicago Cubs. To my left was Lawrence Frank, who seemingly against all odds became an NBA head coach.

Lawrence was now receiving a lot of media attention after he began his NBA head coaching career with the New Jersey Nets by winning his first thirteen games from January 27 to February 24, 2004. That set an NBA record for the most consecutive wins by a rookie NBA head coach. The thirteen-game winning streak was also the longest by a rookie head coach in any of North America's four major professional sports leagues. The game ball was sent to the Basketball Hall of Fame.

I remembered vividly standing in the hallway of Teaneck High School in late 1987 during senior year having a conversation with Lawrence Frank. He stood in the middle of the doorway and leaned against the wide swinging door pinned open with his foot. He was balancing a bunch of books in his arms with a basketball scorebook on top. He asked me what I was going to do after high school. I remember telling him that I had applied to a few colleges and that I eventually wanted to go to law school. When I asked him what his plans were, Lawrence told me that he was going to be an NBA coach. He said that he planned on getting a full scholarship as one of the student managers for the men's basketball team at Indiana University under Coach Bobby Knight. There was a confidence in the way that he communicated this to me that convinced me that someday his NBA coaching goal might come to fruition.

Lawrence Frank was a short, redheaded guy with blue eyes who had always tried out unsuccessfully for the high school basketball team. He decided to become the team manager and kept score and tracked the players' statistics. The only organized basketball that Lawrence ever played was during his adolescent years for a local Jewish Community Center team and as a player-coach for a Catholic Youth Organization team.

I did not think Lawrence ever knew how much I loved basketball, nor was he aware of my friendship with Manute Bol's cousin or that I had hung out with NBA players over dinner at the Meadowlands Hilton just a couple of months earlier. Lawrence and I had a couple of classes together and I saw him around school. However, that conversation we had in the hallway stuck out to me. Just weeks later I had a nervous breakdown and never returned to school. I had enough credits to graduate but never made it to back to see anyone at the high school.

Indeed, Lawrence went on to spend four years as a team manager under Coach Bobby Knight. His decision to learn from one of the best tactical college basketball coaches of all time was calculated. He did the grunt work for the team and whatever they needed done, but it gave him an up close and personal spot to observe the master coach at work and just absorb everything that he could.

With a recommendation from Coach Knight, Frank went on to be a college assistant coach for three years. Later, as luck would have it, one of his mentors, Kevin O'Neill, took an NBA head coaching job and brought along Lawrence as an assistant coach for the Vancouver Grizzlies in 1997. I read this in a tiny article in the back of *The Bergen Record* sports section and was inspired by his accomplishment just ten years from the time he told me that he would be an NBA coach.

In 2000 Lawrence returned home as he was hired as an assistant coach for the New Jersey Nets, which was also my favorite NBA team. The Nets played their home games in the Meadowlands at the arena in East Rutherford just next door to where I lived in Rutherford. I started to see Lawrence in the local area. I attended a radio show broadcast at a Friday's restaurant called "Nets on Tap" where he was a guest. During a commercial break, a Nets employee asked if anyone had any questions. I told the guy that I had gone to high school with Lawrence. When they went live on-air, the host posed the question, "There's a guy here named Jay Gittleson who said he went to high school with you, Coach Frank." Lawrence peered out into the audience, where I was sitting in the back of the room. He said, "Yes, I can confirm that. Jay helped me get through a couple classes." After the show I said hello to him and his wife, Susan, who had also graduated in the same high school class.

One of the speakers I booked was very close to Ray Chambers, who was one of the principal owners of the New Jersey Nets at the time. I was invited to a few special private events held at the Nets

practice facility. There was an annual Christmas party to honor local inner-city kids held there. The entire Nets team, coaching staff,
front office, and owners would attend. I was at the party in 2004 and
spoke to then Nets head coach Byron Scott and told him that I had
gone to high school with Lawrence Frank. He said, "He's a damn
good coach." A few weeks later Byron was fired and the interim
head coaching job was offered to Lawrence.

The following year I was at the same party with my three-year-
old daughter Lizzie. The new owner, Bruce Rattner, was engrossed
in a conversation with Lawrence. I sort of jostled my way into the
conversation by swinging my daughter's legs into his head to dis-
lodge him from the owner for a moment so I could say hello. I had
run into my now famous high school friend on several occasions
and thought it was time to have a meaningful conversation. I started to tell him about the speakers bureau that I had started before
his public relations director approached him with a microphone
and said, "Coach Frank, we need you up on stage to give out some
awards."

As I was leaving the party, I saw him speaking to some friends
and waved goodbye. Lawrence chased me down and told me that
he would be interested in working with me on some speaking engagements, but that his only window of free time was after the NBA
playoffs and before training camp. He said, "I do not do anything
else but basketball during the season. Call me with any ideas you
might have." He looked straight at me with total focus on me and
it felt good and made me feel important. Later in the season I left
a message for Lawrence after the Nets won a game at the buzzer in
Orlando. He called me back the next morning. My office assistant
marveled at the fact that I had received a call from an NBA head
coach.

Lawrence Frank became the winningest New Jersey Nets coach
of all time. His tenure as head coach of the Nets ended in 2009

when his team started an injury-riddled campaign by losing their first sixteen games of the season. He later served as an assistant coach for the Boston Celtics and head coach of the Detroit Pistons for two years, and he had a brief return as an assistant back with the Brooklyn Nets under his former star player turned coach Jason Kidd. Lawrence Frank is currently the president of Basketball Operations for the Los Angeles Clippers.

Trey Lorenz: Singing into a Hairbrush

My first year of college, at Fairleigh Dickinson, was in 1990. That spring of 1991 I decided not to stay in the initial dorm that I was in first semester. I had been friendly with a woman who was vice president of Student Affairs named Judith Kaufman. I spoke to her about moving into another dorm room. She looked into it and found a few open rooms to choose from. I randomly chose this one room that was in another section of the campus called the Wilshires. They were apartments for upperclassmen and fraternities and sororities. The room that was available was on the first floor in the building that housed the FDU campus radio station, WFDU.

I was nervous to go in because I knew that I would have to share the room with someone. The semester had already started so that person by then probably thought they had a single room. As I entered the common area of the apartment it seemed so drab and dingy, as if the people who lived there could care less about the place. There was a musty smell in the outer common area. It had the depressing feeling of an apartment hardly lived in. I felt like turning around and walking out. There were two inner bedroom doors and I decided to look for my room number.

Just then, I heard some R&B music start to play inside one of the rooms. It was really clear and I actually stopped for a moment just to listen to the high-pitched singer. I was starting to enjoy the song, but worried how the person inside the room would receive me. All I knew was that the person's name was Trey. I now knew that he had a really nice sound system in his room. I approached the door and knocked. The door was ajar. I saw an African American guy holding a hairbrush and singing into it like it was a microphone. There was no sound system or radio on. It was the guy singing into a hairbrush. I was amazed. He was pissed.

"What do you mean they gave me a roommate? This is my last semester here. This has got to be some sort of mistake." I told him Judith Kaufman had given me the room number and showed him the paper. He said, "I'm calling Judith right now," so he got on the phone and I felt really bad that I was interrupting his single room and also that I would have nowhere to go. For some reason I did not leave and I just waited as he spoke to Judith. His attitude slowly changed from pissed to inconvenienced as it was explained that I would be his roommate.

Trey started to take apart his large bed, which was actually the two beds in the room put together, so that I would have a bed. It was really awkward. He said he was really busy with a lot of things in his life and in his last semester of college. His goal was to appease his parents, who had forced him to complete his college degree no matter what. Trey told me that he was from Florence, South Carolina and that he always knew that he wanted to be a singer.

He grew up singing in church and had always wanted that to be his career. His parents had stipulated long ago that they would not support him in this dream unless he had a college degree to fall back on. Apparently, he had a cousin who had played for the New York Giants and he suggested Fairleigh Dickinson University as it was close to New York City.

I noticed a full-length poster of Mariah Carey on the wall in the room. It was a pretty famous one from her first album, *Vision of Love*.

Trey went on to tell me that he had met Mariah at a studio recording session and she loved his voice. So, he started singing backup for her at different events. They had become the best of friends. I thought this was really amazing.

I liked Trey, but definitely felt kind of weird staying in the room with him. He usually came in late from recording sessions in the city. He traveled a lot, singing background for Mariah when she appeared on the *Tonight Show*, on *Saturday Night Live*, at the Apollo, and many more. It seemed anywhere she went he was there. One night we sat on the floor of our dorm room and he showed me all of the tapes of his TV performances to date. It was awesome sitting next to him as he narrated all of the videos. I think it was his way of saying thank you for putting up with all of the sleep interruptions and his generally not being the best roommate.

Frequently, his phone would ring late at night. It was usually Mariah. He would ask me to answer the phone and talk to her a couple of times when he went to take a shower so he wouldn't miss the call. My brief conversations with Mariah were cool. "Hey honey, how are you?" Giggle, giggle. I would pretend to be sleeping while trying to eavesdrop on their conversations in the dark from across the room. They talked a lot. One day I asked Trey if he would sign that poster on the wall because I knew he would be famous one day and I wanted proof that I was his roommate. He wrote a funny note to me on the poster: "To my best friend Jay…good luck, Trey Lorenz."

I couldn't wait until the end of the semester to take that poster home. When I moved out of the room, I forgot to take the poster off the wall. I went back the next day to get it and it was gone. The guy who lived in the other room thought it would be worth something and had taken it. He was long gone and Trey had moved out and moved on. All I had was his accountant's phone number that he had given me—Bert Padell. I held on to that scrap of paper wondering if I would ever see or talk to him again.

The following year in 1992 I heard Trey's voice again. It was on *MTV Unplugged* and he was singing a duet called "I'll Be There" with Mariah Carey. It was a remake of the 1970s Michael Jackson version. The song raced to the top of the charts. I was in Florida during Spring Break on a trip that I had won by flying a paper airplane in a contest at halftime of a college basketball game at my school. I started hearing the song on the radio nonstop. Trey had made it.

In the fall of 1992, I went to England to study at Wroxton College for a semester abroad. By the time I arrived in London I saw Trey Lorenz's solo album, *Someone to Hold*, in store windows. Just a year and a half earlier I was sharing a dorm room with him. I thought about that poster that I had left behind. However, on one of my calls home I got some surprise news. My mother was walking in the Columbia University area near where she lived and saw a movie production trailer parked on Broadway. It said "Trey Lorenz in video" on the side of the door. She didn't hesitate and went right up and knocked on the door to the trailer. There she met Trey inside getting his makeup done for a music video shoot for one of his songs on the new album. He was really surprised and welcomed her and thought it was so funny to meet her and how outgoing she was.

The staff in the trailer were asking my mom whether or not her son was in show business and Trey explained that we had roomed together at FDU. My mother went on to tell him the story of the lost poster and how I was studying now in England. Trey grabbed a head shot photo and wrote a letter to me on it and gave my mom a bunch of cassette demo tapes from his new album. A couple of weeks later I received a package in the mail with all these goodies.

In 2006 I got tickets to see Mariah (and Trey) at the Continental

Airlines Arena during her "Emancipation of Mimi" tour. He sang "I'll Be There" and "One Sweet Day" with her and performed several songs on his own during one of her costume changes. As 15,000 fans screamed in the arena, I thought about those nights talking back and forth with him in that dorm room. It was emotional for me to see him perform like that. He had made it.

On July 7, 2009 I had my television turned on to see the Michael Jackson memorial service. As soon as the telecast began I saw Trey on the screen with Mariah at the Staples Center in Los Angeles and they did a special rendition of "I'll Be There."

Trey will always be there to remind me that anything is possible when the right talent meets the right opportunity.

A Vision in Motion

Our daughter Lizzie was born on the first day of the new millennium. She was born smiling! The nurse in the delivery room said, "Quick, take a photo. I have been a nurse here for twenty-seven years and I know the difference between a baby with gas and one that is smiling." After I snapped the photo, my wife went to the recovery area and I was alone in the nursery with my daughter. She was the only baby who was not crying hysterically. She had red hair and chubby cheeks and weighed nearly ten pounds. My life was changed forever.

Becoming a dad was the most awesome thing that ever happened to me. She was the miracle of my life. I truly never thought that would happen for me. When I held her for the first time, I knew that I wanted to make a difference in the world beyond the classroom, where I taught English as a Second Language at an inner-city elementary school.

I had already formulated the idea for a speakers bureau that could address much-needed topics in schools, which included self-esteem and character education, substance abuse and bullying prevention, disability awareness, and conflict resolution. I started to connect with motivational and inspirational presenters who had special qualities and an important message to deliver. I felt like I had put together a super-power team of individuals who had personally overcome major adversity and come out the other side to inspire others. In some ways, I stood on the shoulders of these specially gifted speakers who energized and transformed audiences.

The seeds for A Vision in Motion had been planted in that tenth-grade class taught by my guidance counselor, Mickey, at that private school in New Orleans. I knew what it felt like to be different, alone, confused, and in emotional pain. The bureau soon took flight and I sent speakers to do programs at suburban, rural, and inner-city schools. Someone once told me, "Jay, you have a ministry with sending out all these speakers to make a positive difference in the community."

I not only booked and arranged these programs but often went out with speakers to events at schools, colleges, organizations, and conferences. It became a huge part of my life to see firsthand the positive impact we were having on people's lives in real time.

A gang member was so moved by one of our speakers that he stood up in the middle of a program at a high school in Atlantic City, New Jersey, and gave up his colors to end his affiliation in a gang. It was not uncommon to see big jocks with varsity letter jackets moved to tears by one of our speakers with a disability who touched their hearts. Letters and emails poured in as to how attitudes had been changed, spirits had been lifted, and stereotypes erased.

One of our very first programs on disability awareness was in 2002 at the United Nations' decennial Special Session on Children. We lucked into a private VIP reception that evening for the dedication of the Audrey Hepburn statue in honor of her years of work with UNICEF.

There were many celebrities whom we met in this secure courtyard area including Mia Farrow, Harry Belafonte, Roger Moore, Isabella Rossellini, and Ralph Lauren and a multitude of television networks there to cover the event. I spotted Khofi Annan, UN secretary-general, at the time, whom I so highly regarded. I made my way through the crowd after his speech to see if I could say a few words to him. I got there just in time as his security detail was whisking him back into the office building.

He noticed me and I pointed to my little blue and white UN sticker and explained that my group had done a program earlier in the day. I said, "I want you to meet my speakers from A Vision in Motion." A security guard was leaning on the secretary-general to get inside, but Khofi Annan wanted to stay to listen to me. There was a crush of people between me and my speaker group. It was hard to hear but my last words were, "I would have loved for you to have met them," before I began to make my way through the throng of people back to the other side of the courtyard. I had a suit on and as I made my way through the crowd, I felt someone holding on to the back of my suit jacket. I figured since I was a big guy, I was just helping someone behind me get through. It was the secretary-general riding my coattails along with his wife!

We then had our own private meeting with the two of them. I explained the mission of A Vision in Motion and everyone took turns introducing themselves. I handed the secretary-general my business card, which the security quickly grabbed out of his hand. It was a night to remember.

A Vision in Motion also participated in many youth leadership conferences aboard the Intrepid Sea, Air & Space Museum, the largest naval museum in the world. I was fortunate to get to know the museum's CEO, General Martin Steele, a retired three-star general. I introduced my wife to him at a reception for an invitation-only event during Fleet Week. General Steele leaned in and said, "Your husband has a great mission with A Vision in Motion." I even received a "hometown heroes" mentor award in 2004 aboard the *Intrepid*.

The theme of A Vision in Motion was "overcoming adversity." It was no accident. However, I never shared my personal story until one day in 2018 at a special event at a high school in upstate New York. The event coordinator asked if I could share my story with some of her high school students after a speaker had canceled. I had related to her that I was on dialysis and had a friend who was a possible living kidney donor for me. He was also a speaker so I thought we could share our story of reconnecting as friends in such a meaningful way.

We had three sessions that day at the high school. In the first two programs I shared about my current illness and situation, and toward the end of each session I revealed that my friend was in the process of being evaluated at a transplant center to try and save my life. I was hesitant to really share more deeply about the traumas of my teenage years and why I started A Vision in Motion.

After lunch, I stood in front of about twenty-five high school seniors in a music room. A voice in my head said, *Just go there. Do it. Tell your story.* Something just took over. I started to share my story for the very first time. The students were quiet and very focused on me. My mind and body released something that day from a very deep place in my soul. When I finished speaking, I became very emotional and sat down on a chair in the front row of the classroom and started to weep. My friend walked over to me and whispered in my ear, "Are you okay?" He then turned to the audience and said, "That is the first time I have ever heard Jay's story."

A few students started to clap and then the rest joined in and gave me a standing ovation. It was like a scene out of a movie ending. Afterward, a girl approached me at the front of the room and said, "I don't want that to be the last time you share your story. You should share your story." Another student, who had been very focused on me during my talk, was a big football player with his varsity jacket on. He came up to me and said, "You were my favorite speaker of the day."

I worked on A Vision in Motion all the way through dialysis as much as I could. I decided to reduce my workload in 2019 to focus full-time on finding a living kidney donor. My daughter was always my north star. I wanted to live and to be able to share my story and inspire others and keep that vision in motion.

Mr. October Touches Home

I had already spent two years on dialysis before I transferred to a smaller treatment center in Wind Gap, Pennsylvania. It ended up being my last eight months on dialysis before transplant. I wanted to follow the charge nurse Lorraine, who had been promoted to manager there. She was someone who really looked out for me. It was heartbreaking for me to think about not seeing her again when she got that promotion to become manager of that smaller center.

When I first considered transferring, there was no chair available. So, I waited and a couple of months later a chair opened up. It was suggested that I give it a one-day trial at the smaller center. Apparently, there were a lot of geriatric patients there, including a lady who screamed all the time. The social worker thought it might not be a good environment for me.

I took the chance and went there for the trial day. After just twenty minutes, my mind was made up. It was a cozier center, and even with that lady who screamed all the time, I had a built-in support system there in Lorraine. I was comforted to know she was there even if only as the manager in the back office. The official transfer was completed and I never went back to the other place.

The first thing a dialysis patient did before they started treatment was to weigh in. There was a scale built into the floor. The staff had to know how much fluid someone had gained since the last time. The dialysis machine was then programmed to remove the fluid that was gained in between treatments. When I arrived for my second day in the new center, I went to the scale as usual and weighed in. There was an older man there in a wheelchair near the scale just waiting for a Hoyer lift to take him out of the wheelchair and into his dialysis chair. He was an amputee missing one leg, but he was an upbeat kind of a guy. He said to me, "How long have you been working here?"

"I don't work here. I am a patient here," I said. "My name is Jay."

He said, "My name is Earl, The Duke of Earl." He had bright blue eyes and an Irish-looking fair complexion with spiky, strawberry blond hair. His speech was quick and agile. I noticed a couple of his fingers were partially amputated as well. Earl swung the stump on his amputated left leg up and down. He said that he had just started treatment at the center after having been in the hospital for quite some time.

The charge nurse Lisa came over to me and said, "We are going to put Earl's dialysis chair next to yours and your job is to talk to him and keep him going." In one of our first conversations, Earl told me that he had cancer in eighty-five percent of his body and he really did not think that he had much longer to live.

I asked Earl about his life. He said that he had spent much of his career as a medical professor at several different universities including a couple of universities in China. He was not a doctor, but a director of rehabilitation services and a specialist in exercise physiology. Earl also specialized in the review and certification of the clinical policies and procedures in hospitals.

Earl was eager to tell me about the early years of his life. He had gone to a high school in the 1960s outside of Philadelphia called Cheltenham High School. He said he was one of the few Irish guys in a mostly Jewish area and was quick to tell me about some of the famous alumni of that school. In fact, one of his close friends and classmates was Benjamin Netanyahu, who was living there with his family at the time and went on to become the prime minister of Israel!

Earl also boasted about being a great high school athlete. He had participated in twelve different athletic events through track and field, swimming, wrestling, football, and baseball. Earl had been a great swimmer and had nearly qualified for the 1968 Olympics in butterfly. He told me that while he was a freshman second baseman on the JV baseball team in 1964, Reggie Jackson was a senior on the varsity team.

My mind was blown and it immediately took me back to my own life in October 1977. At the age of seven my favorite baseball player was Reggie Jackson, who played for the New York Yankees. In Game 6 of that year's World Series versus the Los Angeles Dodgers, Reggie hit three home runs, on three consecutive pitches, at Yankee Stadium and became known as Mr. October. I was supposed to have been at that game. My brother's friend, whose family had season tickets, had invited us to the game. As it turned out, only one ticket was left and my more popular brother went without me. I blew up at home and tore apart the house in the biggest temper tantrum of my childhood. I was devastated.

Earl emailed me his resume. It was forty-six pages long with twenty-eight published books. He brought in one of the books and I really promoted him in the center. I was always talking him up about how he had authored all those books and all his accomplishments. I think he liked that but may have been a little jealous at the attention I got from all the visitors I received. Earl was a real stickler for all his medical procedures and would needle the staff for not doing what he perceived to be the right things. He was a little high maintenance.

Eventually Earl transferred to another chair in the center. He developed additional physical problems and was in and out of the hospital. I talked with him on the phone a few times and tried to arrange to meet him for a full interview about his life. It never seemed to work out and eventually he transferred to Monday, Wednesday, Friday treatment days as he wanted to spend more time with his grandchildren on the weekends.

In October 2019, just a short time before I was scheduled for transplant, I had to get an extra treatment at the center. It was on one of Earl's scheduled days. I waited in the lobby after my session for his ambulette to arrive at the center. When I saw him in his wheelchair, he had a beach hat pulled over his eyes. It seemed as if he did not want to know anything from the world. I gently pulled up his hat and Earl was surprised to see me. He looked really worn out, like he was just done. I thought about what I could do to lift his spirits and suddenly Reggie Jackson came to mind. What if I reached out to Reggie and asked him to give Earl a call?

I called my close friend who had some sports connections. He said, "I can get you his cell number. I just don't want you to be disappointed. Reggie is a busy man." I said, "Please get me the number. I want to call him."

I was in dialysis on a Thursday and I called Reggie on his cell phone. Reggie answered the phone and was on another line. I waited patiently and when he came on to the phone I said, "Hi, Reggie. My name is Jay Gittleson and I'm in a dialysis center right now. I'm not calling for business but for a personal reason. One of the guys that I met here, who is very sick, went to Cheltenham High School with you back in the '60s.

"What is his name?" Reggie asked.

"His name is Earl," I said. "He was a few years younger than you and he also played baseball there.

So, Reggie started naming all the guys that he remembered

from his high school team and Earl's name still seemed foreign to him. I said, "Yeah, I understand, Reggie. That totally makes sense because he was four years younger. I just wanted to ask you a favor. Earl is very sick and I thought it would be great if you could give him a call. It would really lift his spirits up."

"Okay. Give me his name and number. I'm going to call him as soon as we get off the phone." I was thrilled and thanked Reggie and told him that I really appreciated it.

I later found out that he had in fact called Earl that Thursday afternoon after we got off the phone, but Earl was resting at home with his phone turned off. However, Reggie had remembered to call back the next day on Friday and he did get Earl, who answered while in dialysis. Earl related all of this to me that afternoon after spending a little over an hour speaking with Reggie on speaker-phone from his dialysis chair and within earshot of patients and staff, who were in awe. Earl told me that Reggie mentioned that a friend from the dialysis center had called him to tell him of Earl's situation. "Was that you, Jay? It really lifted me up."

"Yes, Earl, it was me."

It was nice to think about Reggie's big heart. Apparently, they talked about the old days in high school. Earl was a great talker so I'm sure that Reggie enjoyed it too.

Mission accomplished with a little help from Mr. October.

A Room Full of Love

As my daughter Lizzie approached high school, we sold our home in New Jersey and looked for a new beginning somewhere else. My friend Ron connected me with a speaker who lived in Pennsylvania. As I drove up to the man's home to meet him on a bitterly cold evening in December 2014, a feeling came over me. I was driving alongside a creek and crossed a tiny bridge and up into his development. It felt instantly like this place called Nazareth was where my family should live. We found out that the school system was excellent and moved in time so that Lizzie could start high school there that fall.

When my daughter was in her sophomore year of high school in 2016, I had reached end-stage kidney failure. That fall I met a salesman at an auto dealership while I waited for my car to be repaired. We struck up a conversation as I looked at the shiny new vehicles in the showroom. I told him that we had just moved to the area about a year and a half earlier. He explained that his family had joined together with several other families and started a Christian church in our hometown of Nazareth. Even though I was Jewish and my wife was Catholic, I liked the way he described being part of a tight-knit group of caring and supportive people. I asked if he had a business card for the church. He rummaged through his desk and found one.

I returned a few times to that car dealership for repairs and became friendly with another man in the service department who introduced me to the head mechanic named John who worked on our two older model cars. I related to the service guy Carl that I was on dialysis and could use some help unloading some furniture from a van I had rented. A shiny red vintage Cutlass convertible pulled up into my driveway that Sunday. Carl was in the passenger seat and I was surprised to see John the mechanic was driving. John walked up my driveway and pulled up his shirt as he approached. He showed me two tiny scars near his belly button. I was confused. "Jay, I donated my kidney to my father to give him more time with his grandkids. If you ever need my help to share my story with a potential kidney donor, just let me know. I want to help you."

We were not sure what to expect but about eight months later we decided to go to that church one Sunday. It turned out to be this picture-perfect postcard-looking place just a mile from our home. We had passed that church many times and always remarked how quaint it was. It was an old brick building built in the late 1800s with long, pointed stained glass windows and a white steeple with blue trim that housed a bell tower.

There was a woman greeter at the door who graciously welcomed us. We asked for the man from the car dealership and she said, "I am his wife. Unfortunately, my husband is sick and will not be here." The people were warm and welcoming and it was a cozy place. After the service we met some people in the basement for the fellowship hour over coffee and cake. I spoke with a tall man named John who looked to be in his late fifties. He said that he was a mechanic and eighteen-wheel truck driver who delivered flour to bakeries, restaurants, and stores up and down the eastern seaboard. John also said that he collected clothes and dropped them off along the way to homeless people when he made deliveries in New York City. I shared with John that I had a decades-long friendship with a homeless man in New York City. He listened to me intently and cared about what I had related to him.

Lizzie accompanied us the following week to the church and we felt at home there. I had not shared with too many people that I was on dialysis. One warm Sunday that spring, I had a short-sleeved shirt on and as I entered the church a man said to me, "Did you get stung by a bee?" as he looked at the bandages from my treatment the day before. That was the first time that I said publicly, "I am on dialysis."

The pastor was standing within earshot and suddenly rushed over to me and said, "I want to donate my kidney to you." I was stunned and so touched by his words. He spoke to his doctors but was unable to move forward due to his previous medical history. The people in the church wanted to help me in some way. It was suggested that I should start a Facebook page to share my need for a living kidney donor. Initially I was against it. One person said, "How can anyone help you if you don't tell anyone of your need?"

A couple of weeks later, I received an invitation to a meeting hosted by the Lehigh Valley Hospital transplant center. It was entitled, "Fast Track to Finding a Living Kidney Donor." My daughter and I decided to attend the meeting. When we arrived that night, it was standing room only. A young woman with "Jane" on her name tag approached us at the door and said, "Jay, so nice to see you. Let me get you two chairs." I sort of recognized her, possibly from a previous visit to a doctor's office, but wondered how she remembered my name.

There were many kidney donors and recipients there sharing their stories. A mother spoke of donating her kidney to her son. An older brother shared his experience of receiving a kidney from his younger brother. To me, it was a room full of love.

My daughter and I were especially struck by a man in his late fifties name Kyle, a fifth-grade schoolteacher in Bethlehem,

Pennsylvania, who spoke at length about his instantaneous decision to be an organ donor. A year earlier, Kyle had saved the life of his twenty-five-year-old daughter Kourtney, whose kidneys had unexpectedly failed while she was in her last clinical rotation to earn her doctorate in physical therapy.

Lizzie and I spoke with Kyle and Kourtney after the meeting. I was a former schoolteacher and Lizzie was interested in learning more about a career in physical therapy. We spoke for about an hour.

We were the last people in the room as that woman Jane finished putting all the chairs back in order. I went up to her and said, "Have we met before?"

Jane said, "We met one time at the Access Center. I used to work there."

I asked, "How did you remember my name when we walked in?"

She said, "Jay, you're memorable!"

Jane laughed when I said, "Is that a good thing or a bad thing?"

The meeting was a turning point for me. I decided to start a Facebook page the next day to share my need for a living kidney donor. Kyle became a dear friend who even visited me during some of my dialysis treatments when he was off that summer.

Going to Bat for Me

I had a hard time getting through those long dialysis treatments three days per week. The only thing that took my mind off things was talking to people, but the staff was too busy to engage in very much conversation. My wife petitioned the management of the dialysis center to allow me to have visitors during treatments. Over the next two years, many church friends came to visit me at the dialysis center and helped me get through the five-hour sessions. The support I received was overwhelming. Prayers galore.

In January 2019, a few guys from the church invited me to attend a Christian men's retreat. It was to be held on a Thursday evening, which was a dialysis day. At first, I declined the invitation. I eventually decided to go after much urging and would need to leave right after my treatment that day to meet the group. I knew in advance that the keynote speaker on the first night was Darryl Strawberry, the legendary New York Mets slugger who was named to the MLB All-Star Game every year from 1984 through 1991.

Darryl had overcome many challenges in his life, including drug addiction, colon cancer, and legal problems. He was now sharing his testimony regularly as an ordained minister. My attorney friend Ron had worked with Darryl over the years. He had told Darryl that I would be at the event. I was not feeling well as we arrived at the retreat center right before dinner. There was a buzz in the lobby as lots of people were there to hear Strawberry speak. I looked at my phone and noticed a text from Ron that read, "Darryl wants to see you in his room right now. I told him that you book speakers and he is interested in meeting you. Go to room 206."

I approached Darryl's room and there was a long line of guys already forming down the hallway for the dinner buffet. I knocked and Darryl cracked the door and told me to come in. He was in the middle of getting dressed for his keynote speech. He pulled out the desk chair for me and I sat down as he sat on the edge of the bed to put his socks on. His assistant was sleeping on the other bed in the room.

"Ron told me you book speaking engagements. Tell me more." I told him that I had worked with many different people. "Like who?" I mentioned a few names, which he did not seem to recognize. I wanted to make a connection so I said, "...and Doc Gooden," referring to Darryl's old Mets teammate and friend.

Darryl glanced at the bandage on my arm. I told him, "I am on dialysis."

He said, "I know. Ron told me. I wasn't sure if I could bring that up. You know, Jay, I only have one kidney. My left kidney was removed during my cancer surgery." He tightened his belt and pulled his sweater on. My mind traveled to a story that Ron had related to me. In 2000, Darryl, who was then in legal trouble, had told a judge in Tampa that he had lost the will to live and had stopped chemotherapy. Ron was in the courtroom supporting him. That image appeared in my mind.

I knew that Ron was dealing with some major health issues and that Darryl was now one of the people whom he found comfort in talking to. I told Darryl about the image in my head and I suddenly became very emotional. "Darryl, I'm so concerned about Ron. I love him so much." He said, "You know I've been there for Ron too."

Tears were running down my face.

His assistant, startled, rose off the bed and was looking at me now. I felt that I was distracting Darryl from getting ready for his speech and tried to stand up to leave. Darryl said, "You can't leave yet. We are going to pray. Let's all hold hands." He was so focused on me. In that moment, he was my minister. "Heavenly Father, we pray to you for healing. Encourage Jay on his journey in finding a kidney donor and for his family to have peace of mind." We stood up and Darryl hugged me and said, "Stay encouraged."

Renewed

In March 2019, my friend Phil, who said he would never stop until he helped me find a kidney donor, got in touch with me again. He told me about a Jewish woman named Susie from Teaneck, New Jersey who had been his physical therapist after his hip surgery. Apparently, it was the first time she had ever taken a home therapy case out of her assigned service area and had randomly traveled to the town where Phil lived. In conversation, she learned of Phil's desire to donate his kidney. She told him that she had donated her kidney to save her husband's life several years earlier. After Phil was informed that he could not be my donor, Susie told him, "Don't worry, we are going to help this guy, Jay."

Susie connected me with an amazing organization run by orthodox Jewish rabbis called Renewal. They help potential kidney recipients build a campaign in their home community to find a living kidney donor. Once a match is found, the rabbis guide and support the donor through the process at one of their partnering New York-area hospital transplant centers.

I filled out the application, which included a request for at least two letters from clergy, community leaders, or friends attesting to my character. When I went for my intake interview several weeks later, I brought no less than twelve letters just to be sure.

Once accepted, I worked fast to get listed as a transplant patient at New York- Presbyterian Weill Cornell Hospital. Renewal staff helped me plan an event in my home community for May 6, 2019, where a rabbi would come to Nazareth to educate people on living kidney donation. I needed one hundred people to attend my "Kidney Donation Awareness Event."

I scheduled a time to meet with Pastor Bob in Nazareth to let him know of my plans and to see if he would be able to help me get the word out to people at the church. He asked me to speak at an official church business meeting scheduled for the following week to explain my need. I was so nervous that when I got up to speak, I used up all my time thanking everyone for their support and forgot to tell everyone about the May 6 meeting.

I was so embarrassed and flustered at my failure to communicate the information that I took my coat and darted out of the room. When I got to my car in the parking lot to go to the dialysis center for my treatment, I heard footsteps behind me. It was Pastor Bob, who said, "Jay, don't leave! We all love you." Once I was connected to the machine at the dialysis center, the nurse informed me that I had some visitors. One by one, friends from the church came in to talk and pray with me.

The Bridge of Hope

One Sunday, the pastor asked if anyone else had a praise to share before he started his sermon. Pastor Bob was eager to begin his in-depth and often dramatic Bible analysis.

As he turned to step back toward his lectern, a woman named Jackie—in her early fifties with curly, salt and pepper, shoulder-length hair—stood up. She was not immediately called upon, as the hearing-impaired pastor had his head down and was already opening his notes and adjusting his headset microphone. He finally looked up and saw her but she had already begun to speak. Her voice quivered as she spoke. "I love Jesus with all of my heart. I want my husband to be a believer and have tried so hard to turn his heart toward God."

People seemed a bit taken aback by Jackie's testimony. I saw people's heads turned. I think that Jackie really needed to get that off her chest. It seemed like she really needed a hug and reassurance.

My family had been attending this tiny Christian church in our hometown of Nazareth, Pennsylvania for about a year and a half, from the fall of 2017. The congregation of about sixty to seventy people was comprised of a number of older couples and families who had found a place where they felt that they truly belonged. Even though my wife was Catholic and I was Jewish, we felt welcomed.

I had already been on dialysis for two years at that point when Jackie shared her deeply emotional words. I had spoken to Jackie a few times during the fellowship hour. She was a nurse at a local hospital and had two daughters who were in college.

Many people from the church who had come to visit me at the dialysis center shared some deeply personal things with me. My visitors, who often sat with me weekly during my treatments, shared their own personal problems, relationship struggles, and even thoughts on God, faith, and the church.

Much to our surprise, about six months later we saw Jackie sitting in a rear pew of the church with a man at her side. At the conclusion of the service, Jackie darted my way and was almost hand delivering this man to me. "This is Paul, my husband." He was wearing a T-shirt and jeans and seemed eager to make conversation. I was a little unsure at first as to how Paul would react to me. Our preconceived notion of what Jackie's husband would be like from the way that she had described him did not seem to match up. Paul and I hit it off.

He was funny and easy to talk to. I told him that I was on dialysis. He explained that four years earlier he had been viciously attacked by a man while he was at work surveying a property. Paul was so severely beaten in the head by this deranged man that he suffered a fractured skull and lingering brain damage and was no longer able to work. He expressed to me his love for fishing, painting, and classic television shows and movies. Due to his head injury, he could only drive locally on roads that he knew well because if he hit a bump in the road the vibrations would cause him to have severe headaches and dizziness.

I had just started my 4.5-hour treatment at the dialysis center the following Tuesday after meeting Paul at the church. The nurse told me that I had a visitor. I was not expecting anyone that day. In walked Paul! We picked right up where we'd left off at the church.

He stayed the entire time and even waited for me in the lobby afterward to make sure that I was okay to drive home. Paul continued to visit twice a week and we really got to know each other well. We laughed a lot and it made the treatment time go by quickly.

Paul took me to buy a fishing license and marveled at how I could snag fish out of the local pond. We sometimes went out to eat after my dialysis sessions, and Paul invited me to sit in on a lecture at his art club. We could only travel as far as he could drive around the area as he could not be a passenger in my car due to his head situation. Paul always tried to distract me from the after-effects of the dialysis. We played pinball and air hockey at the local bowling alley, and we sometimes joked around at the order board at the McDonald's drive-thru where his daughter worked.

I was in the process of looking for a living kidney donor when I met Paul. I had just enlisted the help of the Jewish organization that would send a rabbi out to Nazareth to educate my supporters about living kidney donation. Paul invited his family and some of his neighbors to the event and volunteered to assist in any way that he could.

I found an envelope in my mailbox about a week before the event. It had been hand-delivered with no return address and no stamp, only my name. It was a letter from Paul.

Dear Jay,

I know that being on dialysis for so long has been very difficult and has taken a toll on you. It is obviously a very taxing experience physically, mentally and emotionally. Maybe I can relate to you better than most because of the troubles that I've been dealing with. It's easy for me to be empathetic and sympathetic to your situation. I only ask that you continue to be strong and never stop fighting. You and your family deserve your best effort. I feel strongly in my heart that this journey will soon have a very happy ending. Just hang in there until you get the transplant that you deserve. Live in the moment, have hope for the future and don't dwell on the past. Any time you're feeling down, stop by or give me a call. I plan on being your friend for a very long time. Every day since we met, I feel a warmth that I could never have imagined. Whenever we get together, I'm greeted with a friendly smile from a wonderful and caring person. You are definitely unique and all joking aside, I'm saying this in a most complimentary way. I see something in you that I guess many people don't. Your selflessness is the one quality in you that makes you so special to me. Not many people can claim that making someone else's dream come true is their number one priority in life. It is amazing to me that you have not had a lot of friends in your life. People don't know what they've been missing. My mother always said that if you make one good friend in your life you've done well. Thanks for being that friend to me. Your friend forever, Paul

Paul made a beautiful acrylic painting of the bridge that went over the creek into the front of the home where the meeting was hosted. He titled the painting "The Bridge of Hope" because he felt a kidney donor would be found from that meeting. Paul hung the painting in our living room and said that once a donor was found he would give the painting as a gift to the couple who hosted the swabbing event.

Kidney Donation Awareness Event

The pastor and church leadership fully embraced working with the orthodox rabbis who came to Nazareth to educate my home community about living kidney donation. I printed and distributed special flyers designed by the Jewish organization and made posts on social media about my Kidney Donation Awareness Event. I was told that I would need at least one hundred people to attend my meeting. The outreach rabbi's time was extremely precious and he needed to maximize each event to give each patient a chance of finding a match. There were only about fifty to sixty people in the church so I also reached out to neighbors, parents from my daughter's high school swim team, and other people I had become friendly with in the area and followed up to see if they could attend. I did not have a big enough living room to accommodate one hundred people for the event. I asked my friend Al from the church if he and his wife could host the event at their large home down the road and hoped for a big turnout.

When May 6 arrived, I was nervous but hopeful. I received an email about an hour and a half before the start time that the rabbi scheduled to speak that evening had suddenly taken ill and would have to cancel. I was in a state of shock until I got another email that a backup rabbi was on his way but would be late. My daughter and I picked up some specially catered sandwiches and appetizers and went over to the friend's home to set up.

People started arriving for the event. Eventually, cars were lined up as far as we could see leading to the front gates of the home. They just kept coming like in a dream sequence. The image at the end of the movie *Field of Dreams* came to mind when headlights could be seen for miles down a highway in the distance. Those cars were perhaps lined up to fulfill their own magical dream at that field. I wondered if my dream of finding a kidney donor would come true from that night's event.

I was thrust into the role of master of ceremonies. I called upon my friend Kyle, who was there with his wife and daughter to support me, to share some of his kidney donation story. Not long after, two "backup" rabbis had come to the rescue. I met a wonderful thirty-five-year-old Rabbi Moshe, who then took center stage in my friend Al's "Great Room," which he had so aptly named it as it was a great room for me that night. Rabbi Moshe, himself an altruistic kidney donor, had six young children of his own at home. He was funny and inspirational as he educated the standing-room-only audience about living kidney donation.

There were many questions and the rabbi answered them all thoroughly. He explained that at the end of the meeting people would have an opportunity to swab their cheek, which would then be sent to a lab for analysis to see if they were an initial donor match for me. Their mission was to honor the kidney donor. Once a person had been identified as a match, the organization would assist the donor every step of the way. Rabbi Moshe then asked for my daughter to come up to the front of the room, where she met a rabbi for the first time.

I sat in the outside living room area at the conclusion of the meeting. The rabbis set up swab kits on the large kitchen island. Many people swarmed into the kitchen to swab for me. I heard later that the rabbis had brought fifteen swab kits and had run out. They had to mail out extra kits to people. I had no idea at the time that a woman who had swabbed for me had also taken the fifteenth swab kit and put it in her purse to take it home to her husband.

I had a second event at a temple in Teaneck, New Jersey, where I had lived as a young child and later graduated high school and college at Fairleigh Dickinson University. My new friend Susie had put me in touch with Rabbi Ephraim Simon of the Chabad of Teaneck. He agreed to host my second kidney donation awareness event on May 19, 2019, and offered to help in any way that he could. I asked if he could also speak at the event. In fact, Rabbi Simon had donated his kidney years earlier in 2009 to save the life of a father of ten. Then, in January 2019, he donated a lobe of his liver and became one of only a handful of people in the United States to be a dual living-organ door.

My Anonymous Donor

My kidney donation awareness meetings energized me through the support I received from friends and community. It gave me so much hope and took my mind off dialysis. However, as May turned to June and July to August and into September, I heard nothing. Radio silence. By October 2019 I started to lose hope of finding a donor, but I did not want to give up. I thought of my daughter, who was a senior in high school, and wondered if I would make it to her college graduation. I was informed that the rabbi was not available to do a third meeting until the following year. I thought of doing another meeting on my own. Then it happened.

Two weeks later, at the end of October, I received a call from the Weill Cornell transplant center that I had an anonymous living kidney donor! "My donor coordinator, Vanessa, said to me with crackling excitement in her voice, "Congratulations Jay, you have a kidney donor." I froze and could not speak for a moment. It was like taking a gasp of air after holding my breath for so many months. I just could not catch up to my emotions. It was like an out-of-body experience.

I said, "I am getting a transplant?" I believe that Vanessa was waiting for a big eruption of emotion from me but I was very quiet and sort of in shock. I thought to myself, *Am I ready?* I asked Vanessa, "Who is my donor?" She said, "I can't tell you who it is. That is up to the person to disclose or not. I will call you back in two weeks to give you a surgery date but it should be before the end of December." I said, "Thank you for all of your help."

It was about four o'clock in the afternoon. I called my wife to tell her the news. She was in her classroom having just dismissed her students. "Ellen, I have a kidney donor!" She said, "What? I can't believe it." and started crying. She was in a state of shock.

I called my daughter who was in her first semester of college. "Lizzie, I have a kidney donor!" There was a long pause and then I heard some commotion in the background and then heard her crying. I heard other people saying, "Are you okay Lizzie?" Apparently, she had just entered the dining hall for dinner. She was overcome with emotion.

Now, as I awaited my surgery date, I decided to continue planning an event but with the goal of raising awareness about organ donation. I felt compelled to pay it forward and invited patients and families of those still in need of a life-saving transplant to learn more and to be inspired. I invited the coordinators from the local transplant center to share information about living kidney donation as well as a "donor mom" from The Gift of Life to speak about the legacy of her son whose organs helped saved several lives after his untimely death. My now close friend Brian Glennon agreed to be the keynote speaker and to share his experience as a living kidney donor. Phil Aronson, my biggest donor champion, would be the master of ceremonies. The Channel 69 News regional network had agreed early on to cover the event on Monday, November 18, 2019.

Earlier that week, the pastor of the church asked me to share with everyone at the church the good news of my upcoming anonymous donor transplant. I was reticent to share the news at church that Sunday as I felt it would take away attention from the organ donation awareness event the following day to potentially help others. I agreed, though. After all, everyone at the church had been praying for me for quite some time.

As I sat in one of the front pews of the church waiting for the pastor to call upon me to make my announcement, I thought to myself how surreal this whole moment was to finally be able to say that almost three years of dialysis would be coming to an end. However, just as I thought it was my time to speak, a church member named John stood up. He said, "It's kind of a praise and a prayer request all rolled into one. God has kind of put a new ministry opportunity before me. I just want to share it with you."

John seemed a little nervous as he placed a few papers on the ledge of the pulpit. "I want to share a little story that has brought me to this place. Maybe some of you remember a singer-songwriter named Keith Green. He passed away in a plane crash. I think it was 1982. He said something that I've never forgotten. It's kind of comical and profound at the same time. He said, 'Going to church on Sunday won't make you a Christian any more than going to McDonald's will make you a hamburger.' It's true. I have never forgotten this. It's always been a question on my mind. What makes a real Christian?

"I have to confess that a lot of my adult life even after I got saved, I really didn't live as a Christian. There were times when I wouldn't even call myself a Christian. I would say, well I'm a believer in Jesus but to me to be a Christian, the bar is pretty high. It's to be Christlike and I

certainly wasn't living like Christ. So, what does it mean to be a real Christian?"

I always said that John was like E.F. Hutton. When he speaks, people listen. The congregation was quiet and focused and seemed riveted to what John would say next.

He continued, "Well, we can all learn that from the pastor's sermons if we would just practice what he preaches…or we can learn it from the word of God if we practice what he teaches. But for some of us who might be a little hard-headed and stubborn, like me, God needs to put it on display on a great big billboard…and that's just what he did. About three years ago, coming home from a delivery in Manhattan, I was headed up to the George Washington Bridge…and there it was on a great big billboard. The answer I needed to hear. It said, *Real Christians obey Jesus's teachings.*

"So, when the opportunity came for me to go to Haiti, honestly I didn't want to go. My flesh said no. Many people told me I was nuts for going down there and that I would come home with some dreadful disease. But real Christians obey Jesus's teachings. So, I put all my cares on Him and said, Lord, I trust you. I will go and be obedient…and being obedient has its blessings.

It was truly a blessing for me to go there and experience all that I did.

"So, what are some of Jesus's teaching that we're supposed to obey? Well, here's just a short list. Jesus teaches us to go into all the world and preach the good news. The great commission. But we all have opportunity to share the gospel with someone at some point in our lifetime. God puts those opportunities before us. Jesus teaches us to love one another. Sometimes you have to lay your life down for another."

John went on to talk about a tragedy that he had heard on the radio while he was driving in his truck through Massachusetts on his way to make a delivery. He heard about the tragedy of a thirty-nine-year-old firefighter, Lieutenant Jason Menard, who had lost his life in a fire while trying to clear a home from any possible remaining victims. This father of two young children was set to take his family to Disney World the very next day. John started to break down as he related this story of someone "laying down their life" to help others.

John was extremely emotional at this point. I sensed now what was about to happen and I started to cry a little bit. John said, "You can never say thank you enough to our first responders, our military servicemen and women who put their lives on the line every day for us. They provide the safety, protection, and freedom that we enjoy every day...

"So, this new ministry opportunity that God has put before me isn't joining the military or becoming a first responder. I'm a little bit too old for all that but God has called me to lay my life down in a different way."

John directed his wife, Louise, to hand him a small rectangular brown box, which looked like a Christmas gift. It was wrapped in a glittery red bow. John walked over and placed it in my lap. "For You on Your Special Day" was printed in shiny red lettering on the cover of the gift box.

"I want to give you an early Christmas present, Jay." He said, "Merry Christmas, brother. I love you. You are my brother. On Thursday, December 5th, the amazing surgical team at New York Presbyterian Weill Cornell Hospital is going to take my left kidney and make it Jay's left kidney." The church erupted with applause and "awws."

I was already sobbing uncontrollably when I opened the box, which contained a purple plush kidney. The soft kidney also had red, blue, and orange ureter connections just like a real kidney would. One side of the kidney had a black heart-shaped smiling mouth and the other side an upside-down mouth with a sad face. There was also a yellow bookmark inside the box. It read, *God Will Himself Restore, Confirm, Strengthen, Establish Me.* 1 Peter 5:1

I was overwhelmed. In that moment, my emotions took me to some distant places in my mind. I had always craved for security throughout my life. I thought about all the times I was abandoned and how painful that was. My life was flashing before my eyes. Now, someone didn't just care, but they were going to lay down their life for me. John's life-saving gift to me was very hard to handle in an instant. I was crying for my past life and then crying for my new life. John kneeled down beside me with Louise to comfort me. That was all I needed.

As the story goes, John was working and could not attend the swabbing event for me that day in Nazareth, but it was Louise who had taken that fifteenth and last swab kit home and urged him to swab for me. A few days later, when John left on the mission trip to Haiti, Louise mailed in the swab kit. Weeks after his return home, John received a call from Rabbi Moshe, who told him, "You are a perfect match for Jay."

Prayers answered.

The Gift of Life

I sat with my kidney donor John and his wife in the living room of their home as we waited for the car service to take us from Pennsylvania to New York City the night before the transplant. I had three letters, which I handed to John. One was from my daughter, one from my best friend Paul, and one from me. I slowly began to surrender mentally as I thought about the transplant surgery the next day. It was in God's hands now.

The next morning John and I walked together with our wives from the medical hotel just across the street to New York Presbyterian Weill Cornell Hospital to check in for surgery. Our transplant would be the second one that day in the afternoon. My wife and I were soon joined in the pre-surgical room by Pastor Bob and his wife, who had traveled in from Nazareth. John and his wife were across the hall with the rabbi from Renewal. Before I knew it, everyone was in my room. The nurse was a little surprised at all the activity and the party-like atmosphere. I remember, though, wanting to be alone so that I could collect my thoughts.

I went in for surgery on the afternoon of December 5, 2019 and remained in the recovery area at Weill Cornell Hospital in New York City until the early hours of the morning on December 6, which was my mother Sandy's birthday. In fact, my transplant surgeon's name was also Sandy! My mom Sandy could finally remove that blue rubber bracelet from her wrist.

After surgery, I was transported to a private room with a view of the East River. The nursing staff there was amazing and my wife was with me every step of the way. The next day on Friday evening I received my first visitor. It was Dr. H, the psychiatrist I first met at the hospital in 1989 when I was nineteen years old. He was still part of my life. Dr. H was a brilliant, funny, and amazing person. He was only about five-foot-five, but had a huge smile, presence, and engaging personality. He had followed my progress closely over the years. He was more than a doctor or even a friend to me. We were like family. That included his secretary, Frannie, who assisted him in his private practice.

While Dr. H sat on the edge of my hospital bed, the transplant surgeon came into my room to check on me while doing his rounds before he went home. I studied the surgeon's hands and imagined all of the life-saving transplants he had performed. I said, "Dr. Kapur, can I touch the surgeon's hand?" He extended his hand tentatively and I gently touched his fingers and felt the incredible smoothness of his soft skin. Dr. Kapur said, "Jay, can I have my hand back, please."

On Saturday morning, Phil Aronson came to visit me. He had promised to help me get to transplant and he did. I glanced out the door into the hallway and saw my donor John and his wife Louise walking toward my room. John was already checking out of the hospital. After sitting for a few minutes, John approached my bed and put his hand on my belly over my new kidney and said, "Keep working, buddy."

I had told my daughter not to come to the hospital and to focus on her final exams at her university in Pennsylvania. As it turned out, her school had planned a bus trip to New York City that day and she planned long in advance to surprise me. It meant so much to me. She had also informed me the month before that she had decided to go on a birthright trip and left just a few days after my transplant for a ten-day trip to Israel.

My heart was full of joy and relief after surgery. I felt so blessed to be alive and off dialysis. I was told to get out of bed and sit up in a chair as much as I could. As soon as I felt ready, I decided to take a spin around the floor with my IV pole. I put a second hospital gown around my back, grabbed my phone and headphones and took off down the hallway. On my third lap of weaving in and out of staff, patients, and visitors, I realized I may have overdone it a bit. I was alive. My life had been spared.

Tamara's Miracle

I found several kidney-related groups on social media after my transplant. There were thousands of people out there who supported each other with comments and suggestions in response to the myriad questions posed. I decided to post a brief story about my own transplant journey and was amazed to see how many people responded. People seemed inspired and had some follow-up questions and a few of them messaged me privately. I wondered if I could help others with what I knew from my own personal experiences.

I saw a post from a woman who needed a kidney for her five-year-old son. I was alarmed and thought that children had top priority and went right to the top of the organ wait list. Something inside of me wanted to reach out to that mom.

So far, I had just made that one post and placed some smiley faces and heart emojis here and there on these support group pages. Although others had reached out to me, I had not personally reached out to anyone this way through Facebook before about kidney-related stuff. I messaged the mom Tamara and asked her where her son was listed and if I could help in any way. At first there was no response and then I received a message back.

My son does not need a kidney. I need a kidney so that I can be here for my son.

Now I understood.

I could sense she was reticent to engage in a conversation with a stranger so I asked if her husband could reach out to me and gave her my number. I received a message back that she and her husband would like to talk. We spent about thirty to forty minutes on the phone that night. I explained everything I did to find a living kidney donor. I focused on some tangible ideas and resources that had helped me reach my goal of the gift of life. Tamara explained that she was originally from Ecuador and that several of her relatives had tested for her. Her husband said, "Tamara's nephew is a match but he is unable to secure a visa to travel to the United States to donate his kidney to her."

About six weeks later, I received a message from Tamara with a flyer for an upcoming meeting that she had planned through an organization that I suggested. I realized that she had listened carefully in that first conversation and had acted right away. I shared more suggestions on how to maximize her efforts. I arranged for a woman from the church to pray with Tamara and could tell she was inspired especially when she heard the words "Lord we ask for your divine intervention in Tamara's life and that you would do a miracle."

Tamara was so open to it all and was like a sponge now for any ideas that she could implement. I even suggested that she contact her local news network and wondered if that would grab the attention that she needed in the community. I knew that she was determined to find a donor and followed some of Tamara's posts on social media while I went on to assist and encourage other people as well.

About five months later, I received a message from Tamara.

"I wanted to share great news with you. I got transplanted on

May 5th! I am still here in the hospital. I am doing great! My amazing, loving, and caring nephew donated his 30-year-old kidney to me."

I was so overjoyed at the news. It practically lifted me out of my chair. She continued,

"I feel so blessed and I wanted to share it with you. Thank you from the bottom of my heart for all your help during my most difficult days. God bless you always Jay!"

About three months later, I called Tamara to see how she was doing. She sounded great and explained in more detail about how things had worked out in the end after so many challenges. Tamara reflected on her journey and went on to describe how she felt at different stages. She said, "In the beginning, my nephrologist educated me about needing a kidney transplant. But still, after he told me, I was in disbelief. Of course, I was thinking in my head, are these the end of my days? I didn't know what to do. That is when I bumped into you on Facebook. You found me."

I said, "Yes, I remember that day well. I just felt that I needed to reach out at that moment."

Tamara said, "At first, when you contacted me, I was kind of afraid. Then I thought what do I have to lose? You offered to help me. Then I was I like of course. That gave me so much hope and reassurance because now I can hear it from somebody who was in my own shoes. It wasn't that I didn't believe my doctor but sometimes you need to hear it from different people to really grasp it."

"Yes, I know what you mean Tamara," I said. "It helped me a lot too when I was going through the same thing."

Tamara sighed and said, "You gave me a lot of hope and not only that, but I didn't feel alone. It was great to have that outlet and to have that somebody who was sharing things with me and that we can speak the same language. Then, you put me in touch with the organization. That was great and I knew in fact that there was help. You just have to look for it. It was around the time I met you that I had just posted on Facebook and I felt so weird and uncomfortable about it."

"It's hard to open up," I said. "I was like that. Believe it or not. That was me too."

She continued, "I am not the type of person to ask for help and then to ask for a kidney. So, you were so important to me in that process. You gave me a lot of hope and I didn't feel alone. It was just a great feeling. I knew someone was there to talk about it or to walk me through it or to help me to find a donor. I think when we were in that situation it was literally a matter of live or die."

I said, "Yes, in reality, it was like that for both of us at different times."

Tamara took a deep breath and said, "So, to find somebody, a stranger, who wants to help you and cares. That's priceless. I didn't tell you with the months going by. I thought to myself that even if I don't ever find a donor, I can die happy because that feeling when you are in that situation and a stranger helps you. That's amazing because that doesn't happen every day. I don't live expecting people to do things for me. Thinking that way and not looking for the help and just finding the help out of the blue and sincere help. That was priceless to me."

I said, "I'm so glad. It was meant to be."

"I think so too," she said.

I said, "For me, there is a God and things happen for a reason. It's not an accident for me. That's my view of it."

She said, "Yes, I agree. I believe that too. I call the people that really helped me my angels and you are one of those."

Epilogue

After my December 2019 transplant I was ready to restart my life without being dependent on a dialysis machine. In March 2020, just a few days after attending a training in Philadelphia to become a volunteer ambassador for The Gift of Life, the world shut down. Just as I had begun to exhale from the years of kidney failure and dialysis, a pandemic swept the world.

Still recovering from my kidney transplant, I did not get to go back and see friends and staff at the dialysis center. My in-person follow-up visits to the transplant center in New York City ended abruptly. The chief physician assistant (PA) at New York Presbyterian Weill Cornell Hospital transplant, Jehona Marku-Podvorica, became my lifeline. When I had complications, she calmly, decisively, and compassionately walked me through solving each challenge. Jehona led a team of amazing physician assistants. I knew I would be okay when I heard her strong and caring voice on the phone.

I decided again to look outside of myself and started to encourage others on their kidney journeys. I shared information that had been helpful to me in my own search for a living donor and tried to offer emotional support in whatever way I could. These amazing people helped give my life meaning and purpose as I struggled through the fear of COVID and the scary possibility of losing my own gift of life. Eventually, I received some unexpected, moving phone calls from hospital recovery rooms around the country from some of the people I had "walked alongside." They wanted to tell me that they had received a kidney transplant. I was overwhelmed with joy.

My wife worked from home and my daughter returned from college. I opened a memory box of old letters, memorabilia, photos, yearbooks, and journals. It was time to finish writing my book. That was my mission.

I also found that bag of books about many of my sports heroes that my friend Ron had given me when I had visited with him in Florida in 2018. I opened the book *Don't Give Up on Me: Shedding Light on Addiction with Darryl Strawberry*. A typed letter from Ron fell out.

It read, "A year ago you stated, 'Maybe God is punishing me through dialysis' and a year later you are stating that you are meeting and making connections with a lot of different people because of dialysis." Beneath his note was an inspirational quote.

Everything is happening exactly as it's supposed to, with hidden blessings that you'll soon understand. Sometimes what appears to be a problem is actually an answered prayer in disguise. (From Simplereminders.com/McGill Media)

At the bottom of the page it said, "CONTINUE TO BE ENCOURAGED!!!

* * *

I say that my daughter Lizzie saved my life thousands of times by giving me so many reasons to keep fighting and pushing ahead through my long illness. She learned about the struggles and the triumphs of my life through my Reconnection Tour and got to meet many of the people who had made a positive impact on my life. Maybe she saw the best of me in the most challenging of times.

My daughter Lizzie had witnessed my journey through kidney failure and dialysis. She swabbed her own cheek a few months later that summer before she started college to see what her DNA would show about her ancestry. She seemed surprised and excited to learn of her Jewish lineage.

Lizzie left on her birthright trip just days after my transplant. She informed me upon her return that it was "life-changing." I then realized the impact that my unexpected interfaith kidney journey had on my daughter. She had listened, observed, and taken it all in. Her own personal journey inspired me so much. Lizzie helped transport me back to my own Jewish upbringing and the memories of my own trip to Israel.

She made so many new friends and was encouraged by the director to take a leadership role in Hillel in one of the most active student-run organizations on a large university campus. She was ultimately elected president of her Hillel. I had not expected any of this.

* * *

Maria truly became a second mom to me after my transplant. She said, "I am your spiritual mom." She texted me scriptures and we prayed and read the Bible together almost daily as she continued dialysis in New York City during the pandemic. In 2021, she and her family moved to Florida. She has had many medical challenges.

Even through her own illness, Maria continued to support me emotionally and remind me that God still had a plan for me. She said, "He wants you to finish your book. That book is going to bless a lot of people. Maybe they're going through trouble. Maybe they don't believe or maybe they need some testimony that God is real. That's why sometimes when you get down or depressed, I ask God, 'Please touch Jay in a way that he has the strength and wisdom to finish that book.' It's going to be a blessing for a lot of people Jewish and non-Jewish. He has a vision with that book"

She is convinced that the speakers bureau I started after my daughter Lizzie was born—A Vision in Motion—seemed to have been one of the manifestations of her "vision," as it has provided inspirational speakers for over two million school kids and youth on life-changing topics.

It took me several years from the time that Maria and her daughter found me to fully understand the significance of our supernatural connection in 1989. I can see how God had his hand on my life through the darkest moment of a nervous breakdown as a teenager to the greatest moment of becoming a father to Lizzie.

The miraculous people who appeared at just the right moments in my life were my "points of light." They shined so brightly to me as I wrote this book. My life's path could have and maybe should have been much easier. I did not make it to law school to become an entertainment lawyer. However, the universe aligned so that somehow later in life I was reunited on a meaningful personal level with some of the sports and entertainment figures with whom I felt special connections.

Along my journey, the church in Nazareth surrounded my family with love. The rabbis who came to save my life reminded me of my Jewish heritage. I learned about the greatness of humanity in real time through the interfaith effort to save my life. This has led me to frequently and spontaneously turn my palms up to the sky and be in awe of God when I walk each day in the park. When I met John for the first time in the basement of the church in 2017, I felt in some way viscerally that he would one day help me in some way. I am not sure how I could have known that. I do remember that feeling. At that time, I was still a long way from even qualifying to even get on the kidney transplant waiting list and John had no idea of my situation.

* * *

I received a phone call in March 2022 from the nursing home in New York City. It looked like my mom Sandy was nearing the end of life. My daughter and I traveled to see her. She had not eaten in four days and was lying in her bed with just an IV fluid drip. Her eyes were closed. I approached her bedside and gently stroked her arm. She looked up at me and we both started to cry. I put my hand on her forehead and ran my fingers through her hair. She could not speak. I said, "I know, Mom. I know."

Lizzie and I sat with her for a while as she rested. We tried to feed her something to no avail. Suddenly, it dawned on me and I said, "Mom, would you like some matzo ball soup?"

She shook her head yes. We raced over to the kosher deli and brought her back a small container, and Lizzie and I took turns feeding her. She finished it and she came back to life. The next day, I spoke with her doctor, who told me that she was eating all her meals again.

* * *

My almost three years on dialysis had helped me to grow as a person. I have always loved people but there was a special kinship that I felt for my fellow patients and caregivers. We lost some friends along the way. It was not easy. Lisa, the charge nurse in dialysis, had told me that it was my job to talk to Earl, the patient sitting next to me, and keep him going. As I left the center for transplant, Reggie

Jackson had answered the call. I found out later that Reggie kept calling Earl regularly, which was such a blessing for both of them.

Earl passed away in June 2021. I had sent him a final email just weeks before his passing. A few weeks later that June, I unexpectedly received an email from Earl's son Chris, who had been going through his dad's unanswered messages. I had never met any of Earl's family but reached back out to Chris. We spoke for almost three hours on the phone and it seemed that I was able to fill in a few gaps for Chris when I shared the magic of my friendship and dialysis experience with his dad. Chris and I have become close friends and speak often. I call it Earl's "gift" to me.

I had gone from being angry at God to being connected with and feeling his presence in my life. Indeed, God works in mysterious ways.

67506742R00136